THE COLLECTED POEMS OF GEORGE GARRETT

THE COLLECTED POEMS OF

George Garrett

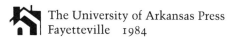The University of Arkansas Press
Fayetteville   1984

Designer: Patricia Douglas Crowder
Typeface: Linotron 202 Trump
Typesetter: G & S Typesetters, Inc.
Printer: Thomson-Shore, Inc.
Binder: John H. Dekker & Sons, Inc.

Library of Congress Cataloging-in-Publication Data
Garrett, George P., 1929–
    The collected poems of George Garrett.
    I. Title
PS3557.A72A17   1984   811'.54   83-4932
ISBN 0-938626-23-X
ISBN 0-938626-24-8 (pbk.)

All my poor heart and my love true
While life doth last I give it you,
And you to serve with service due,
And never to change you for no new.
SIR THOMAS WYATT

In every life sentence
some days are better than
others; even, sometimes,
better than being free.
JOHN CIARDI *Snickering in Solitary*

CONTENTS

III   *Lovers & Others*

Every Bitter Thing

The full soul loatheth an honeycomb; but
to the hungry soul every bitter thing is sweet.
PROVERBS   27:7

ENVOY

Little poem, the two of us know too much.
You and I can never be quite the same again.

I pretend I am gray from worrying over you
while you profess to be concerned about my health.

Walking along together, father and frisky daughter,
holding hands, we are ready to greet friends or enemies.

And I grin, thinking to myself: *You little bitch!*
Nobody else can love you and I couldn't care less.

But you know better: *The old man will eat his heart out,*
ravenous for the love and kisses of strangers.

Cracking and fading like an old photograph,
I am pleased to bequeath the same fate to you.

All supple and shiny now, my son,
you picture my skull and bones on a stone.

You know what happens on the dusty playgrounds,
the raw taste of knuckles, the colors of a bruise.

I know about steppes and tundra of blank paper
and stinking jungles where words crawl like snakes.

Both of us hear voices and believe whatever they say.
In dreams we meet monsters and hold them like lovers.

We shall never talk to each other about any of this.
In all due time I hope to forget your proper name.

Grip tight, little one. Hold your head high.
Strut, you bastard, and smile at the people.

ABRAHAM'S KNIFE

Where hills are hard and bare,
rocks like thrown dice, heat
and glare that's clean and pitiless,
a shadow dogs my heels, limp
as a drowned man washed ashore.
True sacrifice is secret, none

to applaud the ceremony, nor
witness to be moved to tears.
No one to see. God alone
knows, Whose great eye winks not,
from Whom no secrets are hid.

My father, I have loved you,
love you now, dead so many years.
Your ghost shadows me home.
Your laughter and your anger still
trouble my scarecrow head like wings.
My own children, sons and daughter,
study my stranger's face. Their flesh,
bones frail as a small bird's,
is strange, too, in my hands.
What will become of us?
I read my murder in their eyes.

And you, old father, Abraham,
my judge and executioner, I pray
bear witness for me now. I ask
a measure of your faith. Forgive
us, Jew and Gentile, all
your children, all your victims.
In naked country of no shadow
you raise your hand in shining arc.
And we are fountains of foolish tears
to flood and green the world again.
Strike for my heart. Your blade is light.

SALOME

I had a dream of purity.

From weight of flesh and cage of bone,
it was I who was set free
and that other me like a blown weed
was scattered by the wind. Frail bones
(They were so small, so light to carry
that much hunger and fury.)
crumbled into finest dust
and the wind took that away too.
And last of all my mouth, my lips,

4

a red yawn, a taut shriek, my tongue
fluttered like a dead leaf and vanished.
And then it was I who was free,
flying lonely above the ruins,
the slight debris of all the fires
I had lived with, wholly consumed by.
All my dust was gone for good,
and that part of me, the breath of God,
glowed without burning, shone with dark light,
danced like fountains at the weightless peak
of pure delight and fell. . . .

I woke up gnashing my teeth.
—Is anything wrong? they asked.
—Did you have a bad dream?
—Do you have a fever?

—I have had a dream of purity, I said.
And then they all laughed
and my mouth stretched with laughter too,
red and white, obscene,
and my tongue was as sweet as a fresh plum again.
And I . . . I was on fire as before.

I have known other dreams,
the ordinary ones:
Myself naked,
riding bareback on a horse
across a country like the moon.
Something is chasing us
(or *me* anyway)
and my little whip sings
and the horse gnaws at the bit.
The wind is like ice water.
Then suddenly the horse is riding me!
I wake up screaming my name.

Another:
Myself with feathers and wings.
But can't fly. I am caught.
They start to pluck me.
Now each feather is a single hair
yanked by the tender roots.
I try to cry but no sound comes.
My mouth is full of fur.

I wake up and find
I have fallen out of my cold bed.

I tell you all this
not for the pennies of your pity.
Save those coins to cover your eyes.
Nor for your eyebrows
to chevron my rank of shame.
Nor for you to whisper about me
behind your cupped palms.
But that you may know
what a thing it is to be chosen.

I had every right to love and hate holiness.

—What is flesh? you ask.
I have been called sweet,
a hive of dark honey,
worthy of worship
from roots of hair to toes.
I have been called cruel,
the tormentor of dreams,
a dancer of the abstract fancy.
All of which is a dirty lie.
The plain truth is
I was a creature that sweats,
excretes, sags, ages, wrinkles. . . .
My bones were weary of me.

The soul, then?
I think I dreamed it once.

—And the other dreams?
They weren't me. Not me! Not me!
I was not the one who was dreaming.

Bring on the wild man,
bearded like a black sky before a storm,
eyes all alight like white water,
wrapped in rags,
skin and bones corrupted by neglect,
a mouth of ruined teeth and bitter breath,
a cripple cursing every dancer.

—How have you come from my dream?
I wanted to say. —Bless me!

I longed to kiss
but my lips spat for me.

Understand this:
I loved him as myself.
God must love His creatures so.

But I was caged.
My skin and bones hated me.
My thoughts hooded me like a wild bird.

The Dance?
Believe what you care to.
Picture it any way you want to.
All the world knows
truth is best revealed
by gradual deception.
My tongue cried for his head.
But it was my mouth that kissed him
and was damned.

Then I was free and able to rejoice.

A bad marriage from the beginning,
you say, a complete mismatch.
Flesh and spirit wrestle
and we call it love.

We couple like dogs in heat.
We shudder and are sundered.
We pursue ourselves,
sniffing, nose to tail
a comic parade of appetites.

That is the truth,
but not the whole truth.
Do me a little justice.
I had a dream of purity.
And I have lived in the desert ever since.

Because I am broke again
I have the soles of my shoes repaired
one at a time.

From now on one will always be
fat and slick with new leather
while his sad twin,

lean and thin as a fallen leaf,
will hug a large hole like a wound.
When it rains

one sock and one foot get wet.
When I cross the gravel parking lot
one foot winces

and I have to hop along on the other.
My students believe I am trying
to prove something.

They think I'm being a symbol of
dichotomy, duality, double-dealing,
yin and yang.

I am hopping because it hurts.
Because there is a hole in my shoe.
Because I feel poor for keeps.

What I am trying not to do
is imagine how it will be in my coffin,
heels down, soles up,

all rouged and grinning above my polished shoes,
one or the other a respectable brother
and one or the other

that wild prodigal whom I love
as much or more than his sleek companion,
luck's shining child.

MAIN CURRENTS OF AMERICAN
POLITICAL THOUGHT

Gone then the chipped demitasse cups
at dawn, rich with fresh cream and coffee,
a fire on the hearth, winter and summer,
a silk dandy's bathrobe, the black Havana cigar.

Gone the pet turkey gobbler, the dogs and geese,
a yard full of chickens fleeing the shadow of a hawk,
the tall barn with cows and a plough horse, with corn,
with hay spilling out of the loft, festooning the dead
    Pierce Arrow.

Gone the chipped oak sideboards and table,
heavy with aplenty of dented, dusty silverware.
Gone the service pistol and the elephant rifle
and the great bland moosehead on the wall.

"Two things," you told me once, "will keep
the democratic spirit of this country alive—
the free public schools and the petit jury."
Both of these things are going, too, now, Grandfather.

You had five sons and three daughters,
and they are all dead or dying slow and sure.
Even the grandchildren are riddled with casualties.
You would not believe these bitter, shiny times.

What became of all that energy and swagger?
At ninety you went out and campaigned for Adlai
    Stevenson
in South Carolina. Half that age and I have to force
myself to vote, choosing among scoundrels.

THE MAGI

First they were stiff and gaudy,
three painted wooden figures on a table,
bowing in a manger without any walls
among bland clay beasts and shepherds
who huddled where my mother always put them
in a sweet ring around the Holy Child.

At that season and by candlelight
it was easy for a child to believe in them.

Later I became one. I brought gold,
ascended a platform in the Parish House
and muffed my lines, but left my gift
beside the cheap doll in its cradle,
knelt in my fancy costume trying to look wise
while the other two (my friends and rivals
for the girl who was chosen to be Mary)
never faltered with frankincense and myrrh.

Now that was a long time ago.
And now I know them for what they were,
moving across vague spaces on their camels,
visionaries, madmen, poor creatures possessed
by some slight deviation of the stars.
I know their gifts were shabby and symbolic.
Their wisdom was a thing of waking dreams.
Their robes were ragged and their breath was bad.

Still, I would dream them back.
Let them be wooden and absurd again
in all the painted glory that a child
could love. Let me be one of them.
Let me step forward once more awkwardly
and stammer and choke on a prepared speech.
Let me bring gold again and kneel
foolish and adoring in the dirty straw.

IN TUSCANY

In Tuscany
where I was a soldier for a while
the grapes were wonderful on hillsides.
They grew and glistened in the light.
They dreamed all season long
the tuneful dreams of Tuscany.

And they clotted and clustered and swelled
and they spilled over like fountains
green and shining everywhere I looked

until in tidal waves they broke
over the stranded barbwire,
flooding pillboxes, foxholes, and minefields,

stalling tanks and trucks,
disrupting wire communications,
and even carried away the CP tent.

By Christ we got drunk!
We drank and drank
and drank the wine
        of Tuscany.

And reeling in the holy light
        of Tuscany,
I dreamed that all the towers leaned
        in Tuscany.

IN THE HOSPITAL

Here everything is white and clean
as driftwood. Pain is localized
and suffering, strictly routine,
goes on behind a modest screen.

Softly the nurses glide on wheels,
crackle like windy sails, smelling of soap.
I am needled and the whole room reels.
The Fury asks me how I feel

and, grinning, turns to the brisk care
of an old man's need, he who awake
is silent, at the window stares;
sleeping, like drowning, cries for air.

And finally the fever like a spell
my years cast off. I notice now
nurse's plump buttocks, the ripe swell
of her breasts. It seems I will get well.

Next visitors with magazines;
they come whispering as in church.
The old man looks away and leans
toward light. Dying, too, is a routine.

I pack my bag and say goodbyes.
So long to nurse and this Sargasso Sea.
I nod to him and in his eyes
read, fiercely, the seabird's lonely cry.

ENCOUNTER

All the love I had once
(and do not be deceived,
a child's love is miserly
and spent in coins of pain)
was squandered on these
tiny, impeccable, uniformed
soldiers from FAO Schwarz.
In flat thin rectangular boxes,
a neat row in profile, they
came brightly wrapped at Christmas
and on birthdays. Opened,
set free, they stormed to life,
deployed, swarmed and attacked
building-block forts or the high ground
of stacked pillows. O names
and regiments, the Coldstream Guards,
the Grenadiers, the Black Watch and
the King's Royal African Rifle Corps!
Maps and maneuvers and a silent band
with horns and drums and cymbals
whose music set my blood on fire.

I lost them at last, spendthrift
in growing, learning to love
and hate with a Midas touch.
I left the small boy hiding
lonely in the attic with the afternoon's
faint light through the leaves
entering one high window and he
hoarding his meager rich possessions
like a dragon. How do I feel
now, returning where I do not belong—
old pictures, furniture, books and records,
broken toys, trunks of old clothes,
and dust, dust dancing in stale air—

to find the last of them huddled
in a corner, paint-frayed, small
and sad? Golden in the light,
he turns his head to look at me.
"Child," I try to say, "I am even able
to love you now. Let's go downstairs
together." He shakes his head.
His grin is scornful. His breath is fire.

POSTCARD

In my study, blinds drawn, alone
with pen and paper and too many books
I know what happens in my neighborhood
by sounds, by heart. Here comes the milkman,

his tenor engine humming while
the bottles clink a light percussion.
Dogs bark. They start at the other end
of the street until the whole block is a fugue

of snarls. You'd think it was Judgment Day
the way they carry on to greet
the garbage man, laundry man, postman
walking slowly with his little weight

of dooms. That's best of all,
the progress of the postman. I go
with him, sweating, shifting the bag
as I hand over joy and tribulation

or nothing at all, something or other
addressed to the Occupant. He brings bills.
He gives away pleas, rejections, recriminations.
Love and death lie lightly in his hands.

In my study, blinds drawn, alone
with the rhythm of my pulse and the song
of a trapped fly on the window pane,
I write a postcard he can take away:

"Dear World, Though I have loved you
and lost you, times beyond counting,

still I write upon this instant in receipt
of all your ordinary music to inform you

"that I can't live without you.
I intend, by God, hell and high water,
sleet or snow and the wheel of fortune,
to come back to more of the same.

"I am alone too much with too many books,
with blank paper and my cheap fountain pen.
But enough of that for now. In closing
I send you love and kisses.

"When next I appear, blinking, bear from a cave,
I will tell shocking secrets. Turn on
all your power mowers. I'll drown them out.
Let every dog bark! I remain yours truly."

FOR A BITTER SEASON

The oak tree in my front yard dies,
whose leaves are sadder than cheap wrapping paper,
and nothing I can do will keep it long.

Last spring in another place a pear tree
glistened in bloom like a graceful drift of snow.
Birds and bees loved that spacious white

and a daughter was born in the time of flowers.

Now I am a stranger and my oak tree dies
young. Blight without a name, a bad omen.
I die, too, fret in my familiar flesh,

and I take this for a bitter season.
We have lived too long with fear. We take
fear for granted like a drunken uncle,

like a cousin not quite all there
who's always there. I have lived too long
with the stranger who haunts my mirror.

Night in the city and the sirens scream
fresh disasters for my morning paper.
The oak tree in the front yard dies.

Bless us, a houseful of loving strangers,
one good woman, two small boys, a man
waking from sleep to cough his name.

And bless my daughter made of snow and bluest eyes.

REVIVAL

Now chaos has pitched a tent
in my pasture, a circus tent
like a huge toadstool
in the land of giants. Oh,
all night long the voices of
the damned and saved keep me
awake and, *basso*, the evangelist.
Fire and brimstone, thunder and lightning,
telegrams in the unknown tongue!
The bushes are crawling with couples.
I see one girl so leafy that
she might be Daphne herself.

I know there were giants once,
one-eyed wonders of the morning
world. Ponderous, they rode
dinosaurs like Shetland ponies,
timber for toothpicks, boulders for
baseballs, oceans for bathtubs,
whales for goldfish, Great God,
when they shook fists and roared,
stars fell down like snowflakes
under glass! Came then Christ
to climb the thorny beanstalk
and save us one and all.

ARE YOU SAVED?????
Rocks are painted, trees nailed
with signs, fences trampled.
Under the dome of the tent
falls salt of sweat and tears
enough to kill my grass at the roots.
Morning and I'll wake to find
the whole thing gone. Bright dew
and blessed silence. Nothing

to prove they camped here and tried
to raise a crop of hell except
that scar of dead space (where the tent was)
like a huge footprint.

CHILD AMONG ANCESTORS

Dimensionless, they've left behind
buttons, daguerreotypes, a rusty sword
for a small boy to fondle, and the tales
he hears without believing a word

about the escapades of the tall people.
The tight-lipped men with their beards
and their unsmiling women share the glint
of unreality. The facts he's heard,

how this one, tamer of horses, fell
in a flourish of flags and groping dust,
and one who met a dragon on the road,
and another, victim of his lust,

changed into a pig with a ring tail,
fail to convince or bear the burden of
flesh and his struggle for identity.
What he has never seen he cannot love,

though dutifully he listens.
Dismissed, he takes the sword and goes
campaigning in garden and arbor,
and in the henyard mighty blows

glisten in a tumult of feathers.
The hens cackle like grown-ups at tea
as he scatters them to the four winds.
The rooster, ruffled, settles in a tree

and crows an ancient reprimand.
"Let them stand up to me." The boy
thinks. "Let them be tall and terrible
and nothing less than kings." His joy

is all my sadness at the window
where I watch, wishing I could warn.

What can be said of the dead? They rise
to make you curse the day that you were born.

FOUR LOCAL CHARACTERS

1 Loser

Face like an old fighter's
    (that is, hurt)
a bad cough and the color
    of jailhouses
nothing to do with himself
    but hang around
gas stations post office and
    railroad depot
watching arrivals & departures
    yawn like a cat.

Face like Roman stone
    (that is, brute)
chipped and broken nose
    eyes vague
crude hands quick to take
    a cigarette
but too slack to make
    a fist nowdays
Jesus loves him this I know
    who else can?

2 Young Man

Rooster's my favorite bird, the red-combed cock
strutting on drumsticks, a feathered bugle tooting
dark ghosts back to where they belong. Let them
fall in and march away! The sergeant's song
of "grab your socks" cuffs on their baffled ears
like curses, but to mine is brassband prayer.

Let everything be dawning and myself the only Adam
fit to be tried, ready to name the blameless creatures
where they rise from mist to bathe in light
and take for themselves the shapes that God has given

them to wear. I'll bless with a word though I know
to name a thing is not to own it.

Let bugles and whistles and roosters quarrel!
Let stars throw down their spears and run away.
My dogs are loosed to sniff the fox to his den,
and nothing will happen the same way ever again.
I like things loud and clear and sweet enough to burn
my tongue. I pick bones clean, both dark and light.

3 *Holy Roller*

Nothing so white as he is
(not lazy lily nor unlikely unicorn)
when, shirt sweatstained, flapping like
a luffing sail around his ploughboy muscles,
arms outspread like airplanes taking off,
he grins (old piano keys) and hollers:
    "Let us pray!"

I know *your* prayers, brother. I know
why they ran you out of Plant City on a rail.
I know your whiteness is contrived—
eggsmooth jowls, fishbelly hands, ram's hair—
to trouble young virgins where they kneel
and sweetly press their hairless thighs together.
It's your *voice*, dark and hoarse
as a clarinet in lowest register,
that tickles the goodwives where they live.
    Oh, I know you of old, brother.

I know this too:
the ways of God are crazy, daze
a skeptic mind like summer lightning.
Others false and foolish as you (and I)
have been chosen and, so chosen,
babbled more wisely than they knew.
You bow your handsome goathead and
God springs from your lips like a snowy dove.

4 *Wounded Man*

"When all my wounds are healed
and scars are not tender to touch,
I will ride away to the far north

"past spruce and rock and lichen,
beyond the final howl of wolves
to the dry place of purest snow,

"there to train joint and sinew
until my body glows again,
smooth as a fine woodwind.

"God's breath blows a cold tune
as it was in the beginning
and ever shall be, amen.

"I will shape my clay to carry His music.
Oh, I will be back again, bright-eyed,
and singing a terrible new song."

His hands lay open, flat and limp.
He could not even make a fist
to curse me, let alone

grip the reins and ride
the whirlwind to its source
and learn his pain's true name.

PAYMENT IN KIND

Ask me my enemies.
I can fill pages
with their Christian names.

Oh yes I remember
each & everyone of you.
A kiss leaves no scar.

I plan to go bowling
with your hollow skulls
shoot crap with yanked teeth!

I know   I know   I *know*
hatred knots the guts
& anger swallowed

leaves a bitter tongue.
Therefore I dream
the candy of revenge.

Listen! I know your names.
Ask me & I'll answer
damn your eyes.

Let God forgive me.
Isn't forgiveness
His stock in trade?

UNDERWORLD

You've seen coal miners coming up
for air, all in blackface like
no minstrel show comedian,
but bent over, seamed by the danger
and the darkness they must bear,
at once a badge and a wound.

Or maybe a diver on the deck,
his heavy helmet cast aside,
blinking in hard bright light
where every breath's a gust of fire.
It's no laughing matter
to live in two strange worlds.

So it is with certain myths and dreams.
The songs of Orpheus never were the same
after he'd seen hell. They roused
nothing but rage and madness, yet,
after such vision and such loss,
who wouldn't change his tune?

Oh, you'll descend, all right,
dream into fiery darkness or
stumble, awkward among the deep sea
shiftings, troubled by bones
and voiceless cries. And then
you wake and wonder what is real.

Better to come up grinning,
scrub the darkness off yourself,
wisecrack with the ordinary seamen,
unless, like a careless saint, you can
give your soul to God. And then
your flesh belongs to furies.

OLD MAN WAKING

Something hoots.
An owl, a freight train or
a rusty tramp, hull down in harbor.

I wake in a strange land.

Last night I dreamed it all again.
The trees were green as paper money.
The fruit in the leaves was candy
and the grapes had grown so fat and rich
to look at them was to be dizzy drunk.
Birds sang in the leaves and the leaves
leaned together to gossip in whispers.

And you were there
so young and fair
and shining that my heart
like a raw recruit
stumbled to salute.

Then you walked toward me.
The dew on the grass glittered
and the blades of grass parted
before your bare feet like
an armed mob struck dumb
by a pair of fine ladies
naked, soft, and beautiful.

You smiled and offered me a peach.
I ate it all and threw the pit away.
When I looked again
the teeth of your smile were gone
and you were as old as sin.
Flesh of dried figs,
eyes of phlegm,
feet shod in callouses.
Your face went away too,
a smear of candlewax.

I have forgotten your right name.

Something hoots
insistent and derisive
and I wake in a strange land.

I curse the mirror on my wall.
I have lost every key I ever owned.
Now I will dress myself and go forth,
armed with a terrible temper and a walking cane.

Children,
children quicker than birds,
whose eyes are coins of light,
whose laughter is the source of music,
children, come taste my knuckles
and the hard shiny tips of my boots.

EVE

I like the version of Aristophanes,
the story he tells in the *Symposium*,
how we were altogether once and how,
ripped apart, uncoupled, sundered,
we are the lost and naked halves,
and how we dream of that wholeness
as, say, a man who's lost a leg
sometimes feels the joy of his missing limb
springing, dancing, running . . .
and other times he feels it longing
to belong to him again. I don't know
which of these is the greater torment.

The other story, how in dreaming Eden
Adam lost a rib without a wound
and woke to find a stranger he could love,
is too stern for the banquet scene.
I was there. Stood in that garden.
I named the birds, the beasts, the trees.
I tasted the joys of that forbidden apple.
I remember the core was bitter in my mouth
and when I spat the seeds they grew into barbwire.
I heard the thunder of God's kettle drums.
Wounded then, at last, I took your hand.
And we are still together.

VETERANS

"But if the cause be not good . . ."
KING HENRY V, IV.i.

It was a young soldier in King Henry's army
standing by a small fire, warming his hands,
who called up the Judgment Day, that reveille
when all the dead fall in and stand a muster.
He was afraid. He didn't speak
of echelons of angels and the brilliant saints
in open ranks, dressed right and covered down,
but of the mangled, the terribly wounded,
the butchered, slaughtered, with filthy bandages
falling away from scars too cruel to believe.

And on that latter day they'd swarm
to point with stumps and canes and crutches,
calling for justice, all in tongues of fire,
and each would have his holy story heard.
His words danced like ghosts in the dark.
But not a word from veterans. It was cold,
the fire was near and real, and they were warm
for once. (Stars burn, too, but they are far
away.) They will sleep. They will eat,
and in the morning some of them will die.

Oh, on that Day they'll fall us out
at four a.m., field kit and heavy pack.
In the chill dark you stamp your feet and whisper
to the next man down. *This will be a hike.*
The Old Man's fuming. Lieutenants bark like dogs.
"Who's in charge here?" "Move out smartly there!"
We sigh, and then our boots fall on the road
in perfect unison and make a kind of song.
It was the King who prayed. It was
the veterans who shot the killing arrows.

STILL LIFE

An old man at the window looking,
say, like a cloudy moon, his face
pressed round and flat against the cold

glass. Outside a frozen day. Below
he can see his footprints march off
like stout twins and disappear.

Make it late afternoon, the sky
gathering gray around the trees,
the trees a tingle of icy limbs and
supplication which to his mood evoke
the final state of heroes—
dark bones, bright armor, prayer.

Behind him an oak fire, restless
as a dog on a chain, growling of
unspoken possibilities, flickering warm
in the room with shadows like wishes.
But keep him from looking at
the room he knows, a sentence

paused on a dependent clause, a cup
with a slice of lemon bobbing gently
like a painted island in a lukewarm sea.
Let him be silly and human—
pity the twins who got lost in the snow,
sigh while the heroes pray and glitter.

BUZZARD

I've heard that holy madness is a state
not to be trifled with, not to be taken
lightly by jest or vow, by lover's token
or any green wreath for a public place. Flash
in the eyes of madmen precious fountains,
whose flesh is wholly thirst, insatiate.

I see this graceful bird begin to wheel,
glide in God's fingerprint, a whorl
of night, in light a thing burnt black,
unhurried. Somewhere something on its back
has caught his eye. Wide-winged he descends
like angels to the business of this world.

I've heard that saintly hermits, frail, obscene
in rags, slack-fleshed, eyes like jewels, kneel
in dry sand among the tortured mountains, feel

at last the tumult of their prayers take shape,
take wings, assume the brutal rush of grace.
This bird comes then and picks those thin bones clean.

PRAISE FOR A BEAUTIFUL DANCER

—Young willow, willow by the water, why do you bend so
    low?

—To dance in the water and touch the sky.
See how the trout, hunters and hunted,
sway contented in my shade.

—Young willow, why do you let your hair down and
    kneel?

—I am alone and lonely.
The wind is old and cruel.
I kneel and pray.

—Young willow, listener, what do you hear?

—I hear war and rumors of war in the wind.
I hear the hoarse voice of death.
But then I hear the children of the wind,
the small birds singing and singing.
And I have to dance.

EIGHT LYRICS

1 For Narcissus

Hunter in the lonely field,
figure of our primal grace,
all that seems, all that's real,
haunt and lead you on the chase.

The arrow of the heart is keen.
If your hand is steady, true,
reality from the fierce dream,
stricken, can be cut in two.

And triumphantly you pose
beside the victim of your aim
whose frozen features now disclose
the beast you hunted had your name.

2 *For Tiresias*

Speak to us who
are also split.
Speak to the two
we love and hate.

You have been both
and you have known
the double truth
as, chaste, obscene,

you were the lover
and the loved,
you were the giver
who received.

Now tell us how
we can be one
another too.
Speak to us who

in single wrath
cannot be true
to life or death.
Blinder than you.

3 *Dialogue*

"Holy dancer of my skin,
shed the blood and shed the bone.
Leave behind your heart of stone.
Be ruthless and unmesh
     the spirit and the flesh.
               Begin
to dance and live alone."

"I can doubt and I can believe,
am faithless and committed too.
I can deny both false and true,

but really am undone
   to prove that I am one.
                Deceived,
I cut myself in two."

4 Riddle

I am five and I am one:
prophet walking on the sea,
hunter hiding in a tree,
serpent and the holy two.
I am five and I am none.
I am false and I am true.

I am tortured, torn apart.
Self-tormentors I know well,
and for silver I would sell
one of me and seal with kiss
the judgment of a broken heart
and kill myself for less than this.

I am none and I am five.
I stalk the hunter stalking me.
I nail my body to the tree.
I swear and then deny. Although,
flesh and bones do rise alive,
I will doubt myself I know.

5 Reach from Silence

Reach from silence. You will sing.
Like nothing else this music
in untranslated zones
waits for shape and tone
a human voice can bring.

Go armored. No, go nude
as in childhood or at night.
O strip as if for love
to test the meaning of
your crowded solitude.

Wake from dreaming. Like the drowned
float on surfaces of light.
Reach from silence into song

and touch with love what now belongs
to you. Rejoice. Be lost and found.

6 *Lunatic Song*

Under the walleyed moon
  I go where I must
I follow the golden rule
  groping for pale gold dust

Under a smallpox moon
  I shiver like flame
What do you own you fool
  beyond a proper name

and skin I call my own
  and tears that may be mine
of anything under the sun
  but seasoned sticks and stones

What should I praise or blame

Under a stark naked moon
  I sing one note
Give me the proper tool
  so I can cut my throat

7 *Snowman*

A season of the heart can change
  South wind blow warm, north wind blow cold
and what was known be wholly strange
and what was new be old.

All wintered, I am made of snow
  Blow warm south wind, return in flame
and where I am I do not know
and what I've loved can't name.

Return south wind with holy fire.
  Bring green to leaf, bring fruit to bough,
bring birds to sing, turn crowd to choir
where there's no music now.

A season of the heart can turn.
  North wind cuts cruel on bone and brain.
In strictest weather heart can learn
to grope to song again.

8 Hermit

Now on my lips all words grow stale.
I'll sing good-bye a dozen ways.
My father's ghost is wan and pale.
I watch the clock and count the days.

Now on my tongue all names taste dust.
I love the swan, his dying tune.
By hawk and handsaw, ought and must,
I'm troubled in December as in June.

Now in my throat a curse keeps house.
Bless Orpheus, his bloody bones.
Rage is my lawless dreaded spouse.
I can turn sweet bread into stones.

I know a cure for total loss.
Sing farewell night and hello day.
You nail your god upon a cross
and kneel and hear your new voice pray.

PARADIGM

Hand is seized by shape of glove.
Space of birds creates a cage.
Words are anger on this page,
and you are named by what you love.

Heart is where you hang your hat.
Home is core of angry dreams.
The private eye for be is seem.
This is nearer far than that.

Hero's form is wholly stone.
Painted nude is fleshy her.
Place in crowds is most alone.
God is far and near as fur.

Serpent's meaning is the dove.
Fruit is rotten when you eat.
Heart of rage keeps strictest beat.
You are named by what you love.

CAEDMON

All uncompelled, weightless as the notes
rung out of bells at kindling dawn,
more light-thrilled than a rushing stream
over brute rock dashed, these thoughts
flash to song like figures from a dream.

Creation roars. Happens in fire and flood
the riot which is God. A flock of hurts
(the sad crowd, grazing of bitter hearts,
the blank gaze, fright in the rotten wood)
released, reprieved, departs

as, naked, empty as a broken bowl
of everything save light and air, I learn
to praise the water, praise the fire. Burns
then, eternal phoenix, all the soul
I was, and I rejoice to be reborn.

FAMILIAR RIDDLE

What month is this
older than February
greener than envy and money
rich with dark winds
and sudden cloudless thunder?

What day is this
slower than Monday
breathless and completely empty
of birdsongs and sirens
while crowds swarm everywhere?

What age is this
brighter than the Renaissance
and brutal in arts and crafts
abundantly harvesting
tall silos of gold teeth?

What creature is
this stranger beside me
naked and calm as a corpse
yet breathing and speaking
my secrets from a dream?

What child is this
wounded and smiling
armed with a new shiny knife
and flowers for an early grave
who wears my face like his own?

A BARGAIN

Some by trial of fire have failed,
and some in water been swallowed whole,
and some have tried to bed on nails
and some on tightrope taken stroll.

Some from parachute have seen
the earth ascending. Some alone,
from cannon fired, have been
brief wonder, and from stone

a few have broken bread.
This one dodges the cruel horns,
that one falls upon the thorns.
Another rises from the dead.

Lacking a dramatic guise
to test the wisdom of my love
(who's uncommitted can't deny),
I total up the virtues of

the gifted few who in the daze
of glory have risked nothing less
than everything that can be lost.
They take in payment all my praise.

VALUE JUDGMENT

Do not betray me by your smile.
Not with handshake handcuff me,
nor kiss when you should curse, nor be
kind and kill when cure is cruel.

Least of friends are most who grin.
Most of enemies can't grip

so fatally as whose eyes strip
one whole dimension from a man.

The bright queen of the playing card,
jack of hearts who'll give a wink
to anyone are true, I think,
more than flesh that's less than kind.

Who calls me zero, I insist
than enemy is nameless worse.
Who'll bless my name with open curse,
I will salute his sacred dust.

THE VICTIM

Precision's not a virtue. I've seen
the hunter dawdle with the slack
trigger and take aim. I've seen
the fallen beast upon its back.

It is impossible to name
exactly what I've loved. Which or whom
I took from the crowd to tame
have left not monument or tomb.

I know my loves like blood, like bone.
My loves are breath and dust,
are wholly light although my heart is stone.
I am not one that I can trust.

I've seen the hunter squinting at the sight.
I know his breathing and his steady hand.
I know his joy. Have seen my bright
blood spill and blacken on the sand.

DISTANCES, DIFFERENCES

From a tower on a mountain top
I could see five states. They lay
in pools of green and brown and gray
like continents on a flat map

in two dimensions.
I saw them as I saw the land,
level and gentle as an open hand
with not one fist for boundary.

It seemed a kind of eloquence
to be so high and to look down
like angels on the shining lawn
of all that's earthly distance.

I was on a ship once and
the fog closed in like a long sigh.
I couldn't see the sea or sky
and I was far from any land

I had a name for. Eyes
burned out from staring at the sun
must see all differences in one
such shade where facts and lies

like lion and lamb together
huddle in dreaming prayer.
I can love both—the high, keen air,
the ghostly breath of foggy weather.

Logic is something else, a truth
that's all a knotty clenching of
barbwire to shelter what we love
and barricades to keep our wrath.

VIRTUOSITY
(Bernini's Apollo & Daphne)

I see a girl become a tree,
fear cleanly printed on her face,
lips tense with a frozen scream.

From her toes roots reach for earth.
Leaves from her fingers flutter free
to test a breeze which is her clothing.

She is made of marble much like flesh,
veined in blue and polished to a point
where mortal hands are sorely tempted.

Bernini, virtuoso, tortured her
into this being and as well
the slim, lightfooted god a step behind.

I think: What virtue is in this?
Marble is not flesh and blood.
I love the grain of naked lumber.

But here she is, in fact, who first
was stone and now seems flesh
and in one shudder will be wood.

Even the god must be baffled
by richness of change and becoming,
by the anguish of answered prayer.

My prayers stop in my throat.
I dream of lost beginnings.
I huddle in my skin and bones.

Think of Bernini, then. Praise him.
His joyous hands were simply free.
His prayers are songs from Eden.

THE SLEEPING GYPSY

A grammar will teach you how to sing
clause on clause and, in the center
of the knotted thought, the verb bring
home, prodigal in glory, supple tiger

in tame cage displayed. Let fables frame
in excellence their brutal laws.
Know eye and ear are liars, nothing name
that can't be conquered or be shamed.

Far from your dream, your fireside, sleeps
the gypsy, prowls the ungovernable lion.
A guitar is the sum of all its silence, keeps
nothing but music caged; and the wan

moon struggles to be free. This rage
for justice and anarchy of evocation

must be learned. See, like a blank page,
the desert is desire and desolation.

GIANT KILLER

I've heard the case for clarity. I know
much can be said for fountains and for certain bells
that seem to wring the richness from the day
like juice of sweetest fruits, say, plums and tangerines,
grapes and pineapples and peaches. There are so many
ripe things, crushed, will sing on the thrilled tongue.

I know the architecture of the snow's composed
of multitudes of mirrors whose strict forms
prove nothing if they do not teach that God loves all
things classic, balanced and austere in grace
as, say, Tallchief in *Swan Lake*, a white thing floating
like the feather of a careless angel, dropped.

But there are certain of God's homely creatures that
I can love no less—the shiny toad, a fine hog fat in mud,
sporting like Romans at the baths, a mockingbird
whose true song is like oboes out of tune, the crow
who, cawing above a frozen winter field,
had just the note of satire and contempt.

I will agree that purity's a vital matter,
fit for philosophers and poets to doze upon. I'll agree
the blade is nobler than a rock. But then I think
of David with Goliath, how he knelt
and in a cloudy brook he felt for stones.
I like that disproportion. They were well thrown.

A FORM OF JOY

You have to learn the way
the cat, say, or the snake, the hawk,
all triggered, coiled or poised,
yet can be lax with waiting like
a bowstring, gutstring, or
a hangman's neat and empty noose.

You know the tale of cat and mouse.
You've watched a snake retreat
subtly on himself, head up, forked tongue
testing air like a little flame.
You've seen a hawk hang high
on the lucid edges of the wind.

And then you've felt a kind
of chilly blur, furred or feathered,
trim with suppleness, whereby
claw and jaw, fang and talon
fall to seize a form of joy
utterly beyond all telling.

In cloudy languor silent bells
call for your hands to bruise
them into song. Just so
dances the vacant noose, so strung
is bow or violin to catch
your least touch and resound,

rejoice, and startle all creation
with the fury and the beauty of
action struck from pure repose.
Prayer is poise, silence is holy noise.
Be still. Dreaming, a floating hawk
descends like angels to your need.

ADVICE TO AN AESTHETICIAN

Begin with the simple thing,
with, for example, the emotion,
neither expressed nor unexpressed,
hidden or exposed, the abstract,
the unattained, untenable—
the joy of the rose.

Now study it patiently.
Patient as the matador—
philosopher awaiting the horns
of a dilemma. Be brave,
a tireless theologian
tracking God in His cave.

Beginning is discovery
that all creation is a whim,
defined, refined, elaborate
perfection of accidents. So
the enterprise is following
patterns as they go

and come again, detecting
order in spontaneity.
The beautiful is the spontaneous
and unbelievable example—
the rose, its complex poise,
its ample and expected joys.

THE CHILDREN: AN ABSTRACTION

The children,
morning's parables, adapt
a whole day to their rapt
and devious attention. The light,
as yet unbroken, burdens so

this day it swells, explodes
in symbols, and all roads
go straight and shining lead
nowhere but to home.

Choices
are simple in this atmosphere.
Forms are all classical and rear,
clean curve and angle, round and square,
an ample nakedness.

And light, light is everywhere
arranging, improvising, making clear
the contours of wishes, the careers
of least and lost things calling

to begin again. The children, holy fables
on this fictitious day, are fully able
to endure its failing though, prodigal,
the light be spent, the world is torn in two.

PERCÉ ROCK

The gulls, lean knives of soaring,
stop the tourist with a camera
and veering demonstrate an area
of unfixed joy. Here everything
is moving. The sea, at its own speed,
mocks a remote and sweatless heaven
of oblivious blue. The land is driven
backward by a subtle tide.

The gulls trapeze against the sky
and, being innocent and irresponsible,
cut it to pieces. He is not able,
the tourist, armed for tranquility
of home, firelight and family album,
the languid chaos of an uncreated world,
to stop their white destruction. Held
in his hands, the camera is aimed,

records the scene decisively.
But he must turn away and bear
his victory like a scar while sea and air
and world are beautiful with keen activity.

OLD SLAVEMARKET: ST. AUGUSTINE, FLA.

Beneath the fort where Osceola starved
and armored ghosts of Spaniards prowl
for the improbable fountain, a green park,
where this museum piece is standing still

in good repair, is scene of crime.
There, grinning to gloss a savage text,
pale tourists pose and photograph, unvexed
by shady aftertime.

The seabreeze troubles these rich palms
hardly at all. The light that shone
on all our naked fathers will not burn again.

But Truth, distorted, yowls for alms.
Do not go deep, or rotten bones,
yanked into view, will shriek in pain.

SOLITAIRE

The days shuffle together.
Cards again? No, no, I mean
like convicts in lockstep,
like the patients on the Senile Ward
I saw once, gray and feeble,
blank-eyed creatures in cheap cotton,
pumped full of tranquilizers,
("It's the only efficient way to handle
the situation," an attendant told me.)
so lethargic they could hardly pick up their feet.

The gray days shuffle together.
The trees are picked and plucked,
sad tough fowl not fit for stewing.
The round world is shaved and hairless
like the man in the moon. Screams,
but I can't hear it. Next door
the dog howls and I can.
Break out a fresh deck for God's sake!
Bright kings and queens and one-eyed jacks.
Free prisoners. And let the old men go home.

THREE NIGHT POEMS

1 Rome

When the great grey European dark
falls upon the city like a spell,
the streetlights haloed, the old people
huddled in doorways, eyes alert,
and my heart sags in its net of veins
like a rock in a sling (for History
is a giant here, stretches and straddles
the dark continent) and I walk home
and would go on tiptoes if I could
so as not to break fragile anything,
not to kiss dust from anybody's lips
or change anything from stone to flesh,

then always I see the lovers,
the Roman lovers on the sidewalk,

leaning together, he whispering,
she listening, laughing, so close
they can make one perfect shadow.
O Noah's pairs of all creation
couldn't please me more! I hurl
my heart into the deepest night
and hear the astounded giant fall.
And I rejoice. I fumble with my keys
to open doors. I kiss my wife.
I hold my children hostage in my arms.

2 U.S.A.

Say, they roll up the sidewalks all over town
by 11:30 p.m. Lord, by midnight there's nothing
moving, doing. Lone streetlights glare,
one-eyed, but do not dare to dance.
Here and there late lamps burn pale
fire to keep back the beasts of the night.
Somebody's sick, you think (like Huck),
or, less innocent, project the lewd
fantastic, the cheap old beams
and images from broken movies
into frail naked rooms. Alas
for the cop on the corner who offers
a glass-eyed stare, and for the last car
weaving the pavement like a lonesome drunk.
Dancer, giants, heroes and dreamers,
where are you now? It's a fact—
when a heart breaks it doesn't make a sound.

3 Middleclass Nocturne (late 1950's)

My house is thrilled with creaks and sighs,
whimpering shadows, rattling panes,
and twice tonight I've had to rise
to look for prowlers where there are

none but some versions of myself.
My children are asleep. My wife speaks
in her dream. My goods are on the shelf
and hung in closets, safe. And yet I lie

here feeling as I did once, as a child
who dreamed that armchairs stalk the dark

like bears. Wind in the chimney had a wild
tune to play on fretted nerves.

Now there is a difference. Now I know
I'll never teach those bears to dance
or keep them quiet for long. Now I must go
in a cold sweat to find their lair.

And all these things I proudly call
my goods are fragile, perishable, cost
too much. I'll never shrug them all
away to gambol on an early grave.

FOUR AMERICAN LANDSCAPES

1 *Central Florida*

Dark sang all the birds of Florida
in the hush which was like the hush
before sleep, the moment before music.

Everywhere the moon surged. The tide
gnawed at the edges of the fabulous peninsula
and the wind shuffled the palm fronds

like new money. But the real estate
was listening when all the birds sang,
in silence and contemplation and response,

in darkness to the darker song,
renewal (like the moon, the tide),
revival in a logic of echoes and equivalents.

2 *In North Carolina*

In North Carolina
the depth of promise is to learn
how, though the solid mountains lean
in every canting shower, disappear
in subtle fogs, they are still there
and will be for the eyes that keep
appointments with their architecture.

They are always moving, dazed and blue
above the landscape. The cold winds blow

adieus and fanfares through the mizzens
of the timberline, and only lessen,
warmer, on the denser slopes,
the sense that everything is sailing.

Home is lower, looking up,
rapt and amazed to see them drop
deft shadows, which, like breaking waves
deluge the patterned valley, leave
rarely anything afloat, sweep
cornfields and cow pastures clean.

It takes faith to be fixed, to live
with so much happening and prove
nothing and simply be there always
moving and not moving. The truth allows
more changes than one might have hoped,
being perplexed by these perspectives.

3 East River

Then who waking in this golden city
        to see gold coins running on
        the river (and still that prison
        squats there like a rock bird)
        is not astonished as if
        meeting an ugly stranger in a mirror?

4 Fall Landscape, New England

The season fading like woodwind music,
the old leaves flame like falling angels,
I walk on tiptoe amid these muted signs.

Autumn is happening. The mind's anticipation
realized. There's pattern in disintegration.
I am standing in the center of a tidal wave.

Here's dancing for all men who've found virtue
is mostly accidental. Leaves burning and the wind
denies their cries before I can translate them.

He's a liar who sees in this broken color
last spring's polyphonic flowers. Romantic
who revels in promise of more splendor.

White snow, cold tide, soft foam, an idea
in the wind. Trees reach up like drowning men
while worlds go turning to a bitter tune.

PASTORAL

The ghosts of summer learn,
leaning from banks of shade,
how this flowing world, made
holy of breath and dust, turns

always and the seasons shine
like new coins and are spent.
This is the school of discontent
where children of the light define

against a steady tide of dark
the meaning of their banishment
and find on everything the mark
of flood or fire. Not innocent,

there Adam sweats, there Cain raises
his brood of stony hearts. There David,
who downed giants and sang praises,
weeps. There Job composes

his logic of long suffering.
And we, the swimmers, sing
of light and dark who know
so little of so much. Worlds go

and come again, and these waves pound
the living and the dying, leaving
each alone, submerged, fearing
to rise and be counted with the drowned.

THREE MORNING CREATURES

1 Flower

Cloaked, covered, closed.
Light whispered in my ear.

Unfurled, lax to the touch.
Blushed warm as a tongue.
Swayed in my dance.
Breeze only for veil.

2 *Tree*

Sighed, heavy in knots.
Troubled, I took
the posture of prayer.
Blest, my shadow fell
like waterfalls.
Bathed me all day.

3 *Rock*

Couldn't budge.
Heart bitter cold.
Drank heat like wine.
Drunk again. Sprawled,
I winked and settled for
a quiet resting place.

WAYS OF WINTER

How many ways to say this weather?
Think of a ship tormented by pale birds,
a wind all splinters off the world's end
and the cries of gulls like a case of knives.
Picture their cruel maneuvers under
a sky like a great glass eye.

Or call it magic, spell and wand.
Say that one shadow like a lazy hand
waved and changed our green to stone.
All glitters like an antique jewel.
Only a crow can move. He rises
to hover and stay like a dirty word.

Ah, I think we're haunted everywhere
you look. Breathe and a ghost dances
and disappears. "Where's green gone?"
cries the helmsman to the circling gulls.

"There isn't one prince in this bad world,"
whimpers the scarecrow in his trance.

OR DEATH AND DECEMBER

The Roman Catholic bells of Princeton, New Jersey,
wake me from rousing dreams into a resounding
    hangover.
Sweet Jesus, my life is hateful to me.
Seven a.m. and time to walk my dog on a leash.

Ice on the sidewalk and in the gutters,
and the wind comes down the one-way street
like a deuce-and-a-half, a six-by, a semi,
huge with a cold load of growls.

There's not one leaf left to bear witness,
with twitch and scuttle, rattle and rasp,
against the blatant roaring of the wrongway wind.
Only my nose running and my face frozen

into a kind of a grin which has nothing to do
with the ice and the wind or death and December,
but joy pure and simple when my black and tan puppy,
for the first time ever, lifts his hind leg to pee.

MAINE WEATHERS

1 Ice

Dark gulls riding gray air
and every bush and tree and twig
burning wicked as barbwire
every roadway glaring back
every footpath glassy-eyed
each an equalizer where
one and all can dance free and do so
like spastics   like happy drunks
O truth is I have too much loved
too many wrong things for too long
and now my drab and shabby wishes

become a circus crowd of gulls
so lazy   turning so strangely quiet
in the midst of dirty sky
Lord how your glittering rich smile
is everywhere I look around me
among this clumsy dancing and falling
all this our bruising and breaking
Pray unleash now Lord
let sun aloose for just a little while
to melt the rigid glory of your laughter
into our common wages of sweat and tears

2 Gray on Gray

Risen shades   thin shadows   coats and layers
of glare ice   frozen slush   patches of old snow
and the wide slack moronic yawning horizon
shabby waste of woodsmoke overflowing   falling
heavy to be lazy scattered by the pale wind
where I'm walking squinting   leaning into it
breathing it deeply in   myself wrapped in rags
of gray thought   talking to myself
myself a yawning stranger   gray on gray

3 Pathetic Fallacy

Gray thoughts   dark laughter   cold words
and we are old enough to know
better than to take this color   this weather
for our very own   and yet we do
just that   greeting a gray wet day
with the wind out of the northeast
riddled with rain   waves like white feathers
flung across the dark tide   the dark river
while drab gulls soar and circle and cry out
the relentless syllables of pure insatiable appetite
we too swallow this morning whole
grow huge with it   heavy with it

4 How It Is, How It Was, How It Will Be

How it is
on the next day after
the blizzard
how the sky clears   blues   brightens

cloudless and clean with the old moon
floating here and there quiet and grinning
and the quiet fallen snow
glinting   winking   glittering
(is there one and only word for it?)
with abundance   opulence   extravagance
of (one and only) sunlight
how my breath and the river's
do steam and ghost and shimmyshake
in this purely cold air
how now we know
that we shall surely live forever
how now we want to

5 *Early Thaw*

A little sun   a light south wind
and all of a sudden we're in the big middle
of mud season   O long time yet before the lilacs
or anything else   even first green leaves
my loud proud black and tan hound dog
stands to bark at a lone crow high in the dead
limbs of the dying elm next door
Crow shrugs   as only crows can
if crows can   he's lonesome up there all alone
I'm richer owning my own hound dog and also
today all that wrinkling of dazzling gold
on the windy river   as well as
all the fresh thick mud my boots can
gorge and carry   Crow he's a whole lot lighter
if poorer   He can shrug and flap
ragged wings to rise out of the branches
Shrug and flap and fly away   black
as my best thought   a piece of burnt paper
one moody poem too muddy to believe

6 *Holy Week*

Deep Lent and the ratty tag end
of the woodpile has dwindled now
to chips and bark   knots and elbows

Mud and muddy ice   Fog and mizzling sky
Winter is the old world's hacking cough
Birds fight for seeds in my feeder

Not smoke nor any sap is rising yet
Nor anything here can lightly dispell
the weight of this weather within me

Raw and rowdy some reedy jays
trouble the grackles and sparrows
Amazing in bare branches a red cardinal

waits his turn   And so do I
O lead me not into nor leave me be
I who can scold too well enough but never

forgive myself   My boots suck mud
where I stoop and take up rotten wood
to build and burn my latest text of fire

Lord your turn comes next   All alone
on a glistening branch of pain you weep
to see us snarling over these last seeds

7 *Annual Surrender*

Here (again!) an air full of white flakes,
now made of petals and apple blossoms,
fleeing and falling to lie bright and still
like cast away coats on fields of new grass.

Besieged, we learned to hold our bitter tongues,
to cling to a crumbling dust of nothing
in clenched fists. Nailed up lean hopes
like shabby hides on all our doors.

Comes now lord sun with trumpets and trombones.
Come trees with green flags, troops of drunken flowers.
Come forth again these blinking thin survivors,
you and I to (*O!*) open fists and flex our fingers.

To (*ah!*) pick up shining pieces one more time.

8 *Mundane Metamorphosis*

I wake up to discover
that I am made out of lead again
my feet and hands my toes and fingers
are all poured and molded
Even my heart clanks dull and heavy

Dull and heavy I clank to the window
and raise the shade on a bluebright river
with tall masts tilting and bobbing in light
and light gulls tilting on a wide seabreeze
crying out their terrible thin headlines

And all I can imagine is Christopher Columbus
his heart too like a bowling ball
and gulls all around screaming for garbage
being lifted up and easy as a cork on the wave
and seeing then the undeniable green shoreline

Or stout Balboa rusty as an old woodstove
sweat dripping beneath his dented helmet
inching his bulky self up to another limb
then inching his dented helmet above another
whose leaves sigh with his weight and weariness

To see suddenly and always the blue eye of God
which greets his gasp with an enormous wink
The river is burning and the gulls cry doom
but the man of lead now smiles to discover
that even his teeth are rich with silver and gold

9 *York Harbor Morning*

Where clear air blew off the land,
wind turns around and the sky changes.
Where there was burning blue is pale gray now,
heavy and salty from cold open sea.
And the long groaning of the foghorn
saying *change . . . change . . . change*
like a sleeper dreaming and breathing.

Tide turning, too, with the weather.
The lobster boats swing about to pull
against their moorings like large dogs.
Gulls cry like hurt children and disappear.
And I think, surely it is a magician,
bitter and clever, who has pulled this trick.

That old magician is laughing in the fog.
And the cries of wounded children fade away
while the bellbuoy sounds *farewell . . . farewell . . .*
daring the dead to rise up from dreaming,
to hold their lives like water in their hands.

10 Two April Poems

A. FORSYTHIA

Yellow plain yellow
everywhere common
sometimes neat & soft
as a puff of smoke
more often unkempt
extravagant & formless
barbaric & blatant

Yellow plain yellow
not a candle flame
not for heaven's sake
the bold saffron of
Buddhist monks
not even the subtle
shade of daffodils

Yellow plain yellow
when my world's fever
dreaming resurrection
in candy colors & light green
when my world's cold
sweat & cries of thirst
you waken first.

B. ANNUAL COMPLAINT

With spring suddenly outside
everywhere burning everything alive
in green fire & the air haunted
by birdsong & the sky running
away with crowds of drunken kites
& suddenly a swarm of butterflies
living a daylong dream of the sun

> I call it hard labor
> to chase little words
> across a blank page.

11 Summer Thunder Storm
(for R. H. W. Dillard)

Those ancient sisters
who we imagine
imagine they can

50

decide our destinies
with a shrug and a yawn
with less excitement
among them than
the gentle giggling
with which they greet
routine displays
of flatulence
sudden and sourceless
among doily and tea cozy
in their dusty living room
those three sisters
have been dropping
knitting needles of rain
whole drawers and trays
full of gold-plated forks
of lightning
our way all day
not to mention
their older brother
somewhere or other
in attic or cellar
an enraged drummer
deranged tympanist
mad as a hatter
and fully responsible for
those howitzers of thunder
whose rolling barrage
has driven my dog
to take cover
in his safest place
behind the sofa

Sisters your needles
have blinded the dark
eyes of our river
your forked lightning
ripped and rent asunder
our sackcloth of sky
and trees pitch and roll
now tossing now jibing
forlorn in the pelt and howl
while my old house
shivers and shakes

and shudders and now
my old dog whimpers
and I   I curse and rejoice
too   finding and keeping
this ordinary emblem
for fury and frustration
while the rain turns into
mustangs on my roof
and my feet join in changing
into cossacks and clog dancers
and my howls begin to harmonize
with the wind's in the trees

And so I must dance and howl
though I know well enough
the dust and long sorrows
of your cluttered parlor
though I have often studied
the indecipherable texts
and peered at the pictures
in the fading books there
though I know also
how a blue cool day
lazy and theatrical
is already moving this way
from Canada to make of tomorrow
what it will will be   must be
as shining and clear
as white stones in a brook

O believe you me
I know perfectly well
at heart   by heart
how the amazing brightness
is theatrically moving
this way   my way   here and now
to invite me to swallow
my pride and my shame
my fury and frustration
laughing out loud then
when dawn will declare
how my despair and yours
o weary sisters   o witless brother
and even as well the splendid despair

of tragic heroes and kings
will be as if nothing at all
as being purely and only
as brief and foolish
sudden and foolish
after all
as that almost silent fart
which set three sisters giggling

It was, of course,
the dog
who did it.

DANCING CLASS

On certain days when wind and tide and sun
cease their ancient struggles and begin to dance,
the river runs clear and clean again, and I
would drink from it if I didn't know better.

Today there are birds and yellow butterflies,
bumblebees browsing and humming over clover,
and gulls turning and crying above the river,
riding a breeze that teases flags and sails.

My eldest son, my firstborn, lies alone in his room,
home from hard failures, wounded, hoping
the sound of loud music will clear his aching head
of shadows and silt, the pale grin of his own grave.

It is folly to drink. The river water is poison.
Hear how the gulls cry out like cats in the night.
After all our wrestling, our sacrificial wounds,
can father and son ever learn to dance together?

If I could, I would bring him this day like a glass,
window, or mirror, to look into and through,
if only to see himself wink like an angel
or a perfect stranger worth listening to.

AFTER BAD DREAMS

Let holy saints, now safely out
of skin and bones, arise in unison
to tip their hats and halos of pure light.
Let angels dip their wings in flight,
scattering brightness like confusion
of ice and snow. Let poor ghosts shout,

sinners and losers, gray as smoke,
notorious and nameless in this glint
of morning, shout hosanna!
In sleep I walked the desert. Manna
did not fall. I lusted for a hint
of water, tasted dust. A dirty joke

troubled my tongue when I tried to pray.
Yet now there's light enough to swim in
and every stone smells freshly baked.
I drink the wine of morning for my shadow's sake,
he who has suffered and must suffer once again,
who now falls victim to a perfect day.

AUBADE

Let the marvels cradled by this morning grow,
green shoots, beanstalking into the land of knowing
giants who, bearded as Abraham, poor as sheep,
wait for beginnings and the final weeping
　　　which will make them wise.

May morning, to fountain and to fairy tale
aspiring, wholly surviving all clanging
and alarms, become an image of unfailing
promises which, fertile, fruitful, hang
　　　gardens under skies

as clear and cold as silent bells. Praise
for the child, unknown avenger, who
wakes to climbing, climbs to raise
eyebrows in hell and, beautiful, the truth
　　　to shear of all sighs.

ANGELS

There are some things so beautiful
and strange my mind can't hold
them though it wrestle.

An angel sang in Caedmon's ears,
commanded his dumb thoughts to dance
and be articulate.

Sing me creation. And the kettle drums,
the cymbals and the flaring horns
(though they were only words)

made wonders. The words arose
and, winged, ascended into light
where light is music.

The night is cold. The stars,
made brighter in the chill, still move
to tunes I listen for

where I walk, thinking of Caedmon
and of Jacob too, who choked
an answer from his angel.

The trees grasp for it and will be
filled in the morning with singing birds.
I go alone and anxiously

remembering that truth is the center
of all fables and, fabulous,
the lightning of love

creates the angel and the wrestler.
Translate this parable.
It means to praise.

PEOPLE FROM THE MYTHS

1 *Circe*

These are the dancers, my shameless brood,
branch-lithe as March wind, nude as fruit
on limb, and everywhere displayed in shine

of ripeness, the first green, primal gold
of the world, they dance and are all mine.

To be acknowledged or disowned in dreams
each form, enchanted, must be named,
each word, spotlighted, be identified
The words are spells. The forms are built
of flesh. Castled in magic, each prince
is charming and all share equally the guilt.

Springtime is fabulous. You must understand
the nowhere and the nothing it is made of.
Who made this sweating flesh from dust, who
cast the spell? And who can tell the dream
from the dreamy season, love from lust?

Everything is dancing. Tree and toad
from the same darkness spring, and turn
to the same light. Lion and lamb are witness
to this paradox, this music seeking to possess
the purity, tranquillity of blood.

2 *Proteus*

The dangers of recognition are not to be
despised; for even the openhearted who,
rare as mermaids, can sing of surprises and
explicit delights, are threatened by each new
beast, unclassified, night-tossed on shining sand

to be a marvel to children and, to you
and me, disquieting news. To separate the true
from the apparent is a career of daring and
deprivation. It will shake every hand

who thinks of it: How the diver goes below
lonely in zones of slowmotion where
creatures are memory in dissolving shows
of light, and the tinkle of bones picked bare
by time is all the music of the sea.

3 *Adonis*

And on the edge of April when the sun
almost, not quite, is ready to reach
over winter and to touch each
bud and see, mind and buried god,

with intuitions and with ideas clad
in unexpected color, one hopes much.

Hoping is to teeter on an edge
of love, of promising and of decisions
made once and for all, of knowledge
vised in the mind. You vision
all doors opening at your touch,

and, thus corrupted, hoping dies
to be transformed. Gods will rise
and flourish where there was not one.

4 Pandora

How can I judge, see you as you really are,
a slim Pre-Raphaelite girl, a stylized scene
with clean space and a receding procession
of white columns and, ringing your curiosity,
all the raw colors of the world's heart, glare
of the sun like an unsheathed knife, Alpine clouds,
sky in slowmotion like a dream of drowning?

There, alone, a light breeze fondles you
a little, and you toss wishes like a coin.
You lift the lid and hide your eyes.
And then you see the box is empty after all.
You cry a little. And who am I to judge,
seeing we both have stumbled on this knowledge?
The heart of the world has a bitter taste.

5 Echo

Lost before I spoke, I cast
my voice as you might throw
a stone, a ball, some flowers
from a stair. Catch who dares
or cares to. And you shrug.

But stones break bones, the ball
must fall, the bride's bouquet
hovers an instant and
then is torn to pieces.
Hands are so crumbling, eager.

Who calls me? Naked, I crouch
in caves, pray in hollow places,

hurl back myself like fistful coins.
True lovers, good riders, aren't
so easy thrown. *Who calls my name?*

6 *Lament for Daphne*

Loving (we know) is sweet
but leaves a bitter taste
on the tip of the fickle tongue
after the first lie
and the last kiss.

Longing (we know) is bitter,
bed and bouquet of nettle,
crown of brooding thorns,
and one sweet dream
can break all promises.

How shall I weave a pretty cage of words?
My hand is silence, but a name makes noise.

Longing, I call her statue and my wish
to bruise five senses on her bronze.

Loving, I call her holy animal.
(I track to lay a cunning snare.)

Who is caught? Who's free as breeze?
In dreams I print ten fingers on her every inch.

Ghosts crowd my bed, shiver me with sweat.
She dances free, a lightheaded fountain.

Skin is my castle. She is all cloud.
Tongue is my weapon. Her words are leaves.

I think she knows the language of the birds.
I call her tree to praise her sway and poise.

7 *Orpheus*

Spun out of thin air, these fictions
cry for the ears of a believer. Shards
of song fall in shining benediction
on the man who lives in a deck of cards.

I'd like to live always in a shower
of broken glass, in forests where dark flowers

thrive without expectation,
where each wish has its secret destination.

Hidden among angles of the hall
of mirrors, you'll find the answers to
perplexing questions. Words are scrawled
on the washroom wall. They are true.

Beauty, you see, is a stranger to
the beast; they will not meet
nor be identified until the true
from false is stripped, like bone from meat.

To be honest is to witness well.
To be faithful is to trust until
creation sings. While creatures riot,
wait for that chorus and be quiet.

BE UNCORRUPTED ALL

Be uncorrupted all, uprooted quite
from gnarling, grasp and grope.
Be straightened like uncoiling rope
spun whistling over water clean as sight.

Move urgently to mooring. Small
as a shadow, neither monster nor
exactly twin, tugging your toes, sprawled,
a drowned man on the ocean floor

whom tempest and tirade can never reach
to stir to action, torment into song.
In darkness lean towards light. Beseech
new blossomings to happen and the strong

ship, wave-whipped, safely to arrive
in harbor where loves like new leaves thrive.

BACK

Then we were clumsy tourists in our G.I. boots.
Drank grappa, vino, cognac, beer,

and took our time and didn't give a damn.
Drunk, laughing and crying, we staggered among
their ruins (old and new), and when we kissed
our lips touched scars, and where we loved
quiet streets were thoroughfares. "By God!"
said Sergeant X., "I think the German army,
all of it, was here before me!" A pack
of cigarettes, a candy bar was all the key
you needed to their temples and *palazzi*.
Their children whined like puppy dogs,
but what cared we whose children swarmed
unborn? "Kilroy Was Here" we tattooed on
the tender flesh of ancient monuments.
And *Al Ricovero* was the biggest man in Italy.

Now I'm cold sober, lightfooted, armed
with no more than a camera. I take the hand
of my wife to view the vistas and the scenes
our grandparents knew. Their world is with us still.
Vespas and Fiats do the snarling in the streets,
and all the barbwire that I've seen is old.
My countrymen lie peaceful in white rows
here and south along the coast. Mountains
are wonders to look at, not to get across.
How swiftly we have healed! Or so it seems.
"Have you ever tasted grappa?" an American lady
asks me. What can I say? "No m'am.
Why, this is good." And let it go at that.
On the Gianicolo I pass the marble busts
of Garibaldi's fallen men, and in the park
I watch our children grow like stubborn weeds.

DAVID

I think Caravaggio has seen it right,
shown anyway with the boy and the head
(Is it really his *own* face, the giant's,
slack-jawed, tormented? Another story.)
the look of the lean boy, the lips
pursed to spit or kiss, the head held
at arm's length from him by the hair,
the eyes, if they show anything, reading

pity and contempt, hatred and love,
the look we keep for those we kill.
He will be king. Those fingers twined
in dark will pluck the hair of harps,
golden, to sing the measure of our joy
and anguish. By hair will Absalom
dangle from a limb, his tongue a thoroughfare
for flies, and the man grown old and soft
will tear his from the roots to make lament.
The look you give Goliath on that day
will flicker on your weathered face
when you spy bare Bathsheba on the roof
(O the dark honey, liquor of strange flesh,
to turn a head to birds, a heart to stone!)
and you will live to learn by heart
the lines upon this alien face.
So I say that Caravaggio
saw it right, that at the moment when
the boy has killed the man and lifts the head
to look at it is the beginning and the end.
I, who have pictured this often and always
stopped short of the miracle, seen David stoop
to feel for smooth stones in the filmy brook,
the instant when palm and fist
close like a beggar's on a cold coin,
know now I stopped too soon.
Bathed in light, the boy is bound
to be a king. But the sword . . .
I had forgotten that. A slant
of light, its fine edge rest across
his thigh. Never again a rock will do.
It fits his hand like a glove.

THE CHILD ON HIS SHOULDERS
an Italian street fair
For M. A. Peet

There are fireworks as the heavy saint,
held aloft, amid garlands and candles swaying,
possesses, as solemnly as time, the whole street.

There are trumpets and dancing, the odors
of good cooking and all the rich sweat
of celebration. Everything is action, all

things are turning and changing, except
that small child with a pale face, pale as a stone,
fixed high on his father's shoulders.

Taller than any man, he sits above
the burning and the urgency, to see
how strange is joy, how sudden love.

CROWS AT PAESTUM

The crows, a hoarse cone in the wind,
a swarm of flies, so small and busy
they seem, so tossed by breeze
from mountains where the snow
glitters like a brooding skullcap,
the crows, I say, swirl and cry out
and rise to be torn apart in tatters,
a shower of burnt cinders, fall
in one swoop to a perch in the sun
on the lee side of a Grecian temple.

Sheep too. Soft music of light bells.
I have seen them grazing in other ruins,
cropping the shadowed grass
among the broken emblems of empire
and once with the dome of St. Peter's
for background, behind and above them
like a gas balloon on a string.
There behind me posed Garibaldi,
bronze above a squalling traffic circle.
Now crows and sheep and a yawning guard

share the ruins of the Paestum with me.
The wind off the mountains chills
and westward the sea is white-capped too,
is all of sparkling like new-minted coins.
"And they came nigh unto the place
and there builded a great city."
To what end? That a Greek relic

should tug the husband and the wife
from snug *pensione* with camera and guidebook?
For a few tinkling sheep and the exploding crows?

I am uneasy among ruins, lacking
the laurel of nostalgia, the romantic wand,
and cannot for a purpose people empty places
with moral phantoms and ghostly celebrations.
I listen to the soft bells. I watch
the crows come to life again,
sheer off and fall to wrestling the wind,
thinking: "If sheep may safely stand
for that which, shorn and dipped,
is naked bleating soul, why then

I take these crows, whose name
is legion, for another of the same:
the dark, the violent, the harsh
lewd singers of the dream, scraps
of the shattered early urn, cries
cast out, lost and recovered, all
the shards of night. Cold air
strums the fretted columns and
these are the anguished notes
whose dissonance is half my harmony."

RUGBY ROAD
In memory of Hyam Plutzik

I

My days, these days, begin on a road called Rugby,
a rich name summoning counterfeit ivy and distant
    towers
and the loud cries of far-off playing fields
where all the young men, being English
belabor each other in impeccable English
while swans go by like a snowy procession of Popes.

O far from Rugby Road!
Far too from all the sweat and blood,
the grunt and groan and scrimmage of a burly game.

My days begin on Rugby Road
where first light blesses everything
with promises not a living soul will keep.

Now I walk past lawns and houses.
And I in turn am passed by
        by station wagons,
each awiggle with cargo of kids,
each one driven by the same housewife.
She wears a formal painted mask
somewhere between the expressions
of comedy and tragedy.

Ah, lady, I have seen
your nightgown dancing
on the clothesline round with wind.
I have danced with your empty nightgown.
I have hoisted it for my sail
and voyaged like a pirate far and wide,
a fool on the Ship of Fools.
I publish no secrets because
I know only my own.

Now stands above an intricate corner
Mr. Jefferson's splendid imitation of
the Pantheon, here called the Rotunda
and used (the old joke goes)
exclusively for a Rotunda.
I walk through the stain of that shadow
and down the colonnade of Mr. Jefferson's Lawn
and finally meet Mr. Jefferson himself,
seated, wearing a pensive, studious look,
expensive eighteenth-century clothes,
and an excellent patina.

Beneath his gaze, boys in coats and ties
go to and from classes, carrying books,
the weight of all our wisdom in their hands.

I think of Jefferson, the eccentric,
dabbler, gadgeteer and dilettante
high in his crazy castle, Monticello,
which time has also dignified.

A radical who rocked the boat,
who dumped King George and all his tea
into an indifferent sea.

A virtuoso who could turn
pomp and circumstance into a circus tune.
Who tamed and whipped the Lion through hoops of fire.

Time which will tame us one and all,
which can turn love songs into howls,
may yet make music of my groans
or teach me how to sit up and to beg.

2

I am thinking today of the death of a friend,
a poet, a scholar and a Jew
from whom a Christian gentleman could learn
some charity. I have the news today
that he is dead. "He was in great pain,
but brave until the very last
when his mind wandered."

Where does the mind wander?

Do we go all naked and alone
when flesh and worn-out senses fail?
Or are we at last tailored in radiance,
wearing smiles like an absolute shoeshine?

I dream a playing field, all green and Greek,
where plump, conventional nymphs and satyrs roam
and romp with only sunlight for clothing.
(O far from Rugby Road!)

But you, I believe, have found at last
the ruined wall in a dusty place
and kneel there praying for us now.
I would join you there if I dared.

Your prayers are only songs.
Those songs become birds and fly
over the wall and into a sudden garden
where trees are dreaming and fountains play
a bloodless, sweatless game of light and air.

And there one day a bird will sing your name
and fountains begin to dance to that new tune
like young girls veiled in moonbeams.

That shade is far too subtle for my mind.
I do not want to die. I fear
my flesh will make me scream before
it lets me wander where I will.

Better to be a bronze imposter.
Better to wear a coat and tie
and babble of green Greek fields.
Better to hold wisdom in one hand.

I fear I can never make old stones sing.
I fear to leave flesh and bones behind.
I have forgotten how to say my prayers.

3

In the halls my colleagues hurry
to classes, conferences, coffee,
all to the tune of ringing bells.
Bells toll to celebrate beginning and the end
of every fifty-minute session where

we deal out knowledge like a pack of cards.
Perhaps we should wear a cap and bells,
belled mortarboards in honor of
a perilous, ridiculous vocation.

there are no bells in that garden
and the leaves of the trees are laughter

We fear the ridiculous more
than a cage full of lions and tigers.

How can a mind begin to wander free
until at last the last pride of the flesh
falls away like a sad fig leaf?

Leaves are falling here and now
to be raked and turned into smoke.

your fountains are vague as the smoke
and the leaves of the trees are laughter
and the birds in the leaves are songs

and the fruit of the trees is sweet
       and good to eat

Here in a hall the typewriters chatter,
crickets calling in the language of crickets.
And here the unwandering mortal mind
leaps like a grasshopper, tense and agile,
from one blade of grass to another
on the barbered space we call The Lawn.

Some of us are gathering grapes from thistles
and some are busy baking stones for bread.
Our elders doze and yawn like sheiks,
propped on the pillows of reputation.
"Sir, have you seen Susanna lately?
In secret places have you seen
Wisdom, Sapientia, pale Diana,
white and bare as the winter moon?"
They wink and will not answer.

The young lions roar and jump through hoops.
There is a game like rugby going on,
grunts and groans in impeccable English.

4

I envy your open weather, Mr. Jefferson,
the rain and shine, the simple pleasure of
a uniform of painless bronze.
Your words endure in marble places.

I honor you, my dead and buried friend,
whose words exist in slender volumes.

Behind the words the song and dance is free,
free like the birds to fly south from the snow.
South to islands, the richest islands,
where our suntans will be tuxedos,
where girls the color of milk and honey
dance and the breeze is French perfume
and the surf is orchids and ermine
and the roughest blanket is the moonlight.

A bell sounds like a bugle.
I must try to muster my wandering mind.

They are burning up the leaves.
They are burning up the typewriters.
They are folding up their silken tents.

I light a cigarette and reach for a book.
I straighten my tie and grit my teeth
in what I hope and trust will pass
for a polite, uncertain grin.

                              (*Charlottesville, 1962*)

FIG LEAVES

At times sick of the dishonesty of men
to men, the lies that lie in the mouth
like tongues (O the fluttering of tongues
like the snapping of flags in the wind!). . . .
At times sick unto death of myself
and the lies I tell myself, waking, walking,
sleeping, dreaming, lies that must choke
and gag me like a drunk man's vomit
until I lie (indeed) on the ground,
face the color of a bruise, arms and legs
kicking vain signals like a roach on its back. . . .
I could crack my pen in two like a bone,
a thin bone, wishbone, meatless, chewed
down to the slick and bitter surface.
Better my tongue were a dry leaf—
just so dry and crisp, to be bitten to powder.
Better my ears were stone, my pen
at least a hoe, a shovel, a plough,
any good servant of growing things.
Better our sole flag were fig leaves
at least to salute the mercy of God
when in the cool of the evening He came
(Adam and Eve on trembling shanks
squatted and hoped to be hidden)
and cursed us out of the garden.
But not before we learned
to wear our first costume
(seeing the truth was a naked shame),
to lie a little and live together.

68

FOR MY SONS

This world that you are just beginning
now to touch, taste, feel, smell, hear and see,
to have and to hold, and daily more and more
finding sound in your throats, tremors of tongue
to play with, words (some like a ripe plum
or an orange to daze the whole mouth
with sweetness, so that in speaking
you seem to kiss, some like a bitter phlegm
to be coughed up and spit out clean), this world
is all I would claim for you, save you from.

I am a foolish father like all the rest,
would put my flesh, my shadow in between
you and the light that wounds and blesses.
I would throw a cloak over your heads
and carry you home, warm and close, to keep
you from the dark that chills to the bone.
Foolish (I said) I would teach you only words
that sing on the lips. Still, you have to learn
to spit in my face and save your souls
Still you must curse with fever and desire.

Nothing of earned wisdom I can give you,
nothing save the old words like rock candy
to kill the taste of dust on the tongue.
Nothing stings like the serpent, no pain greater.
Bear it. If a bush should burn and cry out,
bow down. If a stranger wrestles, learn his name.
And if after long tossing and sickness you find
a continent, plant your flags, send forth a dove.
Rarely the fruit you reach for returns your love.

EGYPTIAN GOLD

The pickpockets of Rome
are clever as any of their kind
I've ever known. They can
lift a wallet from your pocket
with less touch than the breeze.
They can disembowel a pocketbook

while it hangs, idle, on a lady's arm,
and she'll never notice it until,
home with a sigh, she flings
it on the table where it lies
like a cleaned fish. And when
they work in duets and trios,
as for example at the *Stazione Termini*,
it's with the precision of ballet.
They thrive on difficulty.
Button your coat, hold onto your purse
like a new baby, and nevertheless
your property is theirs if they
have a mind to take it.

But private property isn't
our proper topic just now.
I don't own much, it's true;
and it isn't likely that either
pickpockets or poets
will ever be rich enough to care.

The point is:
what happens when you fall among thieves?
And who, Lord, is my neighbor?
Jesus Christ, who knew one thief
from another, had the answer
for a lawyer to ponder on,
a hard saying. There is just one
Samaritan. The rest of us
lie naked and beaten in the ditch.
Now, in an age when thievery
is so refined it calls itself
Success, when to be stripped and beaten
is to be foxed, when all grapes
go to the vineyard keeper,
and nobody, early or late,
draws any wages, and we applaud
the blind man leading the blind,
I feel like saying with P. T. Barnum—
"This Way To The Egress!"

But then I must call to mind
Saint Augustine glossing *Exodus*,
explaining why God gave permission
for Moses to take along Egyptian gold

and showing how this means
that all things belong to God.
And if we are going to build
new temples we might as well
use the marble of the pagans.
And if we're going to tell the truth,
we'd better gut the pocketbooks
of all the poets who tried and failed.
As we pass by their honored biers,
we'll pick the pennies from their eyes.

I'm pleased by the Roman pickpockets.
As I said, they never get really rich,
and finally their fingers lose the art,
stiffen out of subtlety
(just as sweet singers grow hoarse).
And they end up wistful on corners
watching a new generation strut
sassy and unplucked past them.
As long as they don't get my passport,
I'll praise them and their skill.

But I don't want to leave the impression
of an American overseas
and overawed by all that's foreign.
My grandfather lost his good gold watch
in an elevator at the Waldorf.

II

Bubbles & Others

And therefore, Hoost, I warne the biforn,
My joly body schal a tale telle,
And I schall clynken you so mery a belle
That I schal waken al this compaignie.
CHAUCER   *Epilogue of The Man of Law's Tale*

LITTLE MOVIE WITHOUT A MIDDLE

The big bad abstractions are back in town again.
Tall, slope-bellied, shaded by wide-brimmed hats,
dragging their huge shadows by the heels, they swagger
down the empty street. A hound dog rises from his snooze
near the swinging doors of the Red Eye Saloon and slinks
        away
without even pausing to stretch, boneless as poured water.
Chink-a-chinka-chink, bright spurs warn the dusty world.
Beneath an enormous sombrero, a Mexican crosses
        himself,
and then continues to snore more loudly than before.
Acting more on inspiration than logic,
the Sheriff pins his tin star on the Town Drunk
and runs to catch the last stagecoach for California.

Meanwhile into a sunny plaza ghostly with fountains
here come generalizations in full dress uniforms,
all lavish in polished leather and brass buttons, tilting,
nearly topheavy with medals, these brilliant officers
of the old regime. *Oompah-oompah-oompah* blares a
        band
while the crowds wolf down bananas and chocolate bars,
buy every balloon and pound palms raw with sweaty
        applause.

Now cut directly to the inevitable moment
when the smoke is finally clearing away and there they
        are,
heels up and spurs down, those generalizations,
hanging conventionally from the streetlamps and phone
        poles.

Their rows of medals make a tinkly music.
See also, flat as oriental rugs along the street,
those are abstractions who once were fast on the draw.
While buzzards circle like homesick punctuation marks,
the simple and specific common nouns come forth again
to clean up mess and mark the spot for scholars
        (*oh oompah-oompah, chinka-chink*)
with a row of gravestones grinning like false teeth.

LITTLE TRANSFORMATIONS

Leaving the cocktail party
I steal the Admiral's hat
At home I try it on
See how much it changes me

Now I am purely different
I am handsome I am jaunty
I have pride and power on my head

Let him be sad and ashamed
Let him curse himself and whoever took it
Let him feel hopeless and lost without it
Let his wife laugh in his naked face

Listen Admiral it fits me fine
It looks just right on my closet shelf
My family will preserve it in my memory
My future history will be worthy of it

Sir I thank you kindly for it
And I solemnly promise never to stand
downcast and shifty in front of anyone
with your hat humble in my hands

FAT MAN

O flesh, my tyrant wife, my shrew,
old slattern, what's to become of you?
Of us? It's true I've come to hate
the way you smirk from mirrors, float
in steaming tubs, sweat on summer days
or, shameless, writhe in nets of eyes
that measure all your bulk and girth.
It's you I love although I curse your birth.

What is to love? To love's to dance.
The spirit leads the flesh. Without a wince
the flesh should follow and should smile.
A map of all of you shows miles
of frowns. I study you and weep
for pity's sake—the only crop I reap.

76

I'll never leave you, cruel and fair,
who leave me panting halfway up the stair.

ROMANTIC

I've heard some jealous women say
that if your skin were cut away
and tacked upon a public wall
it would not please the eyes at all.

They say your bones are no great prize,
that hanging in the neutral breeze
your rig of ribs, your trim of thighs
would catch no fetching harmonies

but tinkle like a running mouse
over piano keys. They hold
that, stripped, your shabby soul
will whimper like a vacant house

you are so haunted. "Ask
her," they say, "if she'll unmask.
Let her shed beauty like winter trees.
Time will bring her to her knees."

Still, I must have you as you are,
all of a piece, beautiful and vain,
burning and freezing, near and far,
and all my joy and all my pain.

And if you live to scrub a floor
with prayer, to weep like a small ghost,
which of us will suffer more,
who will be wounded most?

RAPE OF THE SABINES
a frieze in the Roman Forum

It seems to be a kind of dance,
graceful, almost stylish in the way
two of the victims are carried high,

slight ballerinas swooning in the arms
of men whose grip is less than gruff.

One is running, sure enough.
She's half-naked already, and real harm
is a step and the length of a hand away.
Though he will have her by and by,
there's a hint of pleasure in her wince

as if she acted in the trance-
like state of dreams where dire alarms
are set to music. My grownup's eye
is a ghostly witness. Play
of children is composed of just such stuff

and nonsense, threat and bluff.
We may have been a race of dancers once,
I think, before we tried to come to terms
with what is truth and what is clearly lie.
We went stark naked night and day.

Now it's mere folly to obey
an impulse just to stand and sigh
(at whose doors some real wolves huff and puff)
for that lost childhood and its charms,
its equal parts of rape and sheer romance.

BUBBLES

Not like we used to with pipes
which combined the pleasure of
pretending we were smoking with
the chance of a mouthful of soap.

But nowadays with a sea-green liquid,
bottle, and a spoon-shaped eyelet
with a handle. You dip it
and in one wave you have

a room that's full of bubbles.
Round and rich they catch the light
in square small patches of color.
And they hover, float and fall

and pop. My children are
pleased and puzzled. It is new
to them. They snatch at globes
to find their hands are empty

and the bubble's gone.
Let some stern moralist take on
the task of making sense of this.
I never could explain why balloons

burst and playing-card towers fall.
I say they're beautiful to see,
however made, by pipe or wand,
and not to have.

Kings might have given ransom
to own an air so jeweled and clear,
so nothing-filled and handsome.
Children, there are no kings here.

WONDERFUL PEN
(A Snapshot)

When I bought this wonderful pen this morning,
at Ulrich's on South University in Ann Arbor,
the lady escorted me personally to the checkout counter,
maybe because I might try to sneak out without paying
but also because it was clearly a kind of an occasion
for me and for her and (I guess) for the store.
After all, how often does someone just walk in here
and ask for and pay cash for a $185 fountain pen?

The lady tells the girl at the cash register
what the pen costs and that I get a faculty discount
of 10%. Casually, then, I peel off and plunk down
four $50-bills, poor old U. S. Grant on the front of each.
It is payday, and I am feeling good, feeling fine.
I have been saving a long time for this stubby black Mont
        Blanc
with its bright gold nib which is sure to teach me some
        golden words.
I smile. Girl glares back her altogether savage disapproval.

"Jesus Christ!" she exclaims. "People are starving in
    places like Bangladesh!
They are killing each other with clubs in Uganda and
    Cambodia!
And you—I can't fucking *believe* it!—are spending a
    fortune
on a fountain pen! What can you possibly *do* with a pen
    like that?"
Saddened, embarrassed, but refusing to feel guilty, what
    can I say?
"Lady, this pen takes moving pictures; it records human
    voices and
if you stick it all the way up your ass, you'll find that you
    can sing
more sweet songs than a canary or a Georgia
    mockingbird."

SOME SNAPSHOTS

1 *Italian Lesson*

When I hear of the death of another major poet these days,
I remember Rome, 1958, myself standing alongside an
    enormous priest
by a newspaper kiosk in Trastevere, staring at headlines—
IL PAPA E MORTO! As the priest turns away a voice from
    the crowd
(all too poor to buy a paper) calls out: "Is it true the Holy
    Father is dead?"
The priest nods, then shrugs hugely and answers in the
    local dialect:
"Better him than us, eh? Better him than us." And walks
    off to his chores
among the poor who are always with us even until the
    end of the world.

2 *Ambassadress*

We had a parade for that lady near Livorno.
I spent a solid hour shining on my boots.

We got there and lined up,
    eight thousand men,

and waited quite a while because she was late.
Finally she showed up and rode up and down
trooping the line in a white jeep.
She said America would be proud of us
and what an important job we'd done in Trieste.

After it was all over and we were back in the tents,
a man in my squad (he was from Alabama) asked me:
"Say, Sarge, who the hell *was* that Clara Bell Lou
    we fell out for?"

3 Politician

When I went to the funeral
he was more solemn and tiptoeing
than even the undertaker.
    For Christ's sake!

He had a great big hand and a good word
for everybody. He was driven in
an air-conditioned Cadillac.

His hair was black, luxuriant and curly
    as the wool on a ram.
And when he *did* smile it was like all the lights
    of a Christmas tree going on at once.

At the grave, just after the coffin was lowered
(it went down so quickly, quietly, it was astonishing),
somebody asked him about a speeding ticket.

"My word's good as far as the Savannah River,"
he said. "After that you're in the hands
    of Herman Talmadge."

SPEAKING OF MINOR REVELATIONS
(David & Goliath)

What could be virtue in a giant
is rashness in small boys. The point
beyond which childhood is
calamity is clearly marked.

The giant, standing like a bear,

must be astounded, raise a roar
of natural indignation or
tilt back to laugh at the improbable.

So they must always meet that way,
be disciplined and neat as puppets.
And so I must always praise,
with brutal innocence, the accidental.

He's lucky who dies laughing
in the light of it, who leaves
the deft philosophers to argue
that excess is illumination.

COME AS YOU ARE

Who can't be passionate and brave
dressed like a musketeer, a sly
rapier taut along the thigh?

Who's as erotic as the slave,
the white one, she whom the sheik's
least oriental gesture turns as weak-

kneed as a new calf? Here's
Antoinette, the sport-
ing queen and, there, the short

man's idol, a Napoleon
of bangs and a hidden hand.
All in this company may comprehend

the joys of Proteus, the complex
piety of masks, a face
that's not for long. Without a trace

survivors of shipwreck disappear,
replaced by grinning cannibals. Forget
not yet the Space Cadet,

he to whom moon and stars
are near and known. Nor
ignore Eve whose leaves implore

an Adam to be tempted one more time.
(The hopeful pathos in her eyes
is not concealed by her disguise.)

All pity's in the aftermath:
costumes for mothballs, gilt
by water gone, a sword at hilt

clean broken. Who believes
that gods in flesh have changed
the dead to quick, familiar to the strange?

FROM THE ACADEMY

1 Sir Guy of Gysbane
(For the grad students—past, present, future—at Princeton)

Springtime and the leaves like a green lace,
yet thick and warm as tongues calling his name,
when Sir Guy came at last into the strange country.

His armor was rusty, wore the scars of flame.
One eye was bloodshot, the other patched,
and if he smiled, his mouth was a ruined fence.

Nothing out of all his stern experience
popped (jack-in-the-box) to help him understand
what he was seeing—the horses gaunt, the men
as thin and quiet as shadows and
so broken, so crippled, so hurt,
that even he felt oddly whole.

There were sights there to break his heart
(that which has been called a thing of stone
by more than one gnashing set of teeth),

and now, tired out and all alone,
he felt bones trickle and blood go cold,
for first time ever knew the sweat of fear.

"What are *you* doing here?"
Cried a stranger on a sagging crutch.
But another offered him a wooden hand.

"Welcome, Sir Guy, to your native land.
Don't be afraid," he (smiling) said.
"We are all wounded in this place."

NOTE   Sir Guy of Gysbane is an imaginary Medieval figure—
soldier, scholar, statesman—created by the gradgrinds, myself
included, at Princeton. At first we used him to plague aging pro-
fessors with oblique references to his canon and career. Later he
was used, like a left-handed monkey wrench or a bucket of
polka dot paint, to trouble the new students. They searched in
vain for him in the dim stacks of the library. Finally, he became a
symbol (perhaps Sisyphus would have been a more accurate one)
for our labors. I've always liked Sir Guy.

2 *General Prologue*
For D. W. Robertson, Jr.

Outside the classroom dogwood snows
extravagantly pink and white.
The students are tracking Chaucer as he goes
on pilgrimage this season, as he must

yearly spring up to lead by hand
the wary and unwary toward
a Middle-English promised land.
The students doze and nod in April days.

Well, there's a robin on the path
all ready to be transformed into
that heavy-breasted wench, the Wife of Bath.
There's calm in this brightness to recall

Griselda, patient and perfect as a stone.
And there's the fever of the dogwood to
shiver them wholly, skin and bone,
which, in the same way, shivered Alysoun.

Fixed in a time of ice and fire,
of dancing flowers and the singing chord
wind plucks from the strings of my desire,
lost in the quick profusion of the light,

I think: "Only the dead
can be untroubled when the trees
are burning brightly and each stone
is turned into a loaf of bread."

3 Milton's Adam

He first was all alone.
      Birds flashed in air
      and everywhere
bright creatures moved like smoke
in a light wind. Spoke
not to him nor tree nor stone.

He first knew loneliness
      who could not move
      toward any love
or by such learning be
hurt or whole. He
first of all touched emptiness.

He first was wholly lost
      dreaming her face,
      the form in space
her flesh would fill, her breath
of language and the death
that his duplicity would cost.

4 Congreve

Nothing is lost or won.
The sun shines as it has to
on the just and the unjust.
Rain falls on the false and true,
and what was beautiful is dust.

But wit, the amazing virtue,
"that sparkles while it wounds,"
endures now in the dance,
your parry and thrust of words
fenced in formal elegance.

We've become accustomed to
barbwire, the searchlight glance,
explicitly indifferent,
and order's rare as innocence
viewed by victims of discontent.

This much has been proved:
the distance from here to truth

is light-years, reckoned by
wit or learned in wrath.
" 'Tis better to laugh than to cry.' "

5 *Swift*

Swift has been misunderstood, his rage
called everything but honesty,
the buzzing in his brain identified
as everything but the lightning of God.

Now scholars nod over the burning page,
with pencils poised, fidget and warble
their footnotes wild, and Stella is
and she isn't, and God knows

Swift had marbles in his head—
tall sculptured figures posing there,
naked and shining, the image of
the rare and endless possibility of man.

Follow him, if you can, with eyes
wide open. Sketch for a skeptic age
the contours of his anger and his love.
But humble if he, furious, replies.

6 *Charlemagne*

Always the tall king in the mosaic must
from that coined light come to life
and, like yourself, myself, assume the dust
of three dimensions, fret of flesh.

There is another. The tamed past
like a bear on a chain can move
to music if the music lasts
and execute the dance of rage

controlled. In the astonished eyes
of children he must live it all again,
from sparkling significance arise
to be only an old man on a horse

riding to Roncevaux too late;
from there turn north to find his place
in stone or glass and prove the state
of time's amazing currency.

7 Matthew Arnold

I think, after all, you were right.
The whole man is a man divided,
Adam and the glory of his wound
doubled to beauty in a single night.

And how shall we live with ourselves?
Shall I follow my inner dancer
or assume the logician's poise of stone?
You, once expert to answer,

smile across years and the changes
even the Critic never dreamed of,
let alone the Poet, a stiff Greek
gesturing for pity and for love.

But, troubled like the rest of us,
you found a voice and gave a name
to what you loved. If now
there's only smoke where there was flame,

if ancestral notions tumble down
and critics, having been deceived
too often, drop their pens and run,
there's still the strict example of your frown

to shame them back into the ranks.
Adam, torn in two, discovered,
strange and beautiful, another self
to live with. He gave thanks.

8 My Version

Enter a very odd man
heart of gravel and his head
filled with outrage and straw

Dogs slink away from
the path of his shadow
Where he leaves footprints

briars and thorns arise
to choke the roses   Rain
falls around him fore and aft

She in her tower
is lonesome and happy
A slow-motion smiler

she can with a wink
turn even hay meadows
into blocks and banks of gold

"My name," he begins. . . .
"I already know," she says
sweeter than a marshmallow.

"I have heard this story
too many times. Tell me
what took you so long."

Rumplestiltskin shrugs
weary and eloquent
as an ox under a yoke

"It's no joke,"
he answers, "to be notorious,
to find myself always so

lost in the wrong tale of woe.
Listen, Lady, the woods are burning
with charming Princes

who appear to be certain
that you, my Princess,
are sound asleep and dreaming."

Now it's her turn
and she can shrug more lightly
than any butterfly

"There's no trick
to waking up," she explains.
"But dreaming is pure magic."

"Pardon, did you say tragic?"
"Ah, what Prince has half the charm
of your average sad-faced clown?"

"Have a heart!" he cries.
"Okay, let's pretend
I don't know you from Adam,"

she replies.

9 *The Metamorphosis of Professor J . . .*

While studying the habits of the rose,
he disappeared, banished into thinnest air,
it seemed, leaving no trace. A rare
meticulosity, triumphant nose,
and marvelous unruly hair
are strangely absent from this atmosphere.
What is his substance now, do you suppose?

I've heard it said that he became a bee,
a nuzzling, droning thief of sweet and bright,
fumbling near the heart of things, and quite
properly armed. (His prose, you see,
was wicked, though the tone was light.)
Winged, he can indulge an appetite
for truth and sting his critics literally.

His enemy suggests he is a worm.
"He always was a crawler, don't you know,
happy to chew a rose to shreds, to show
even perfection has a little term,
its time to flourish and its time to go
to pieces. He'll have *his*, though.
Impaled on a fisher's hook, he'll learn to squirm!"

Neither, I think, is fair or true.
I do not know, myself, what he became,
but like to think he found a finer frame
than flesh and was transformed into,
say, something he loved. Without a name
he's free of both our praise and blame
and keeps his secret as the roses do.

10 *Professor of Belles Lettres*

His book-lined study ought to be a TV set.
Some very nice first editions in alphabetical order
    and himself fully armed by J. Press,
chainsmoking while he conducts a class—
"The Growth of National Consciousness in American
    Lit."

There's a picture window with a view
of barbered green lawn and a man with a lawn mower.
"Italians love to cut grass," his wife said.

Afterwards there is tea
during which he collects
the latest undergraduate slang
in an indexed notebook.

I do not know if he believes in anything
or has any love by which he lives,
but, over the shine of the teacups
and the glint of the silver service,

have seen tears in his eyes
when he talked about Sacco and Vanzetti
        or the peace of Walden Pond.

11 *Gadfly*

At the Faculty Meeting I saw him bleed
for Nonconformity and, good classicist, bare
all his wounds, calling on us to rise, rebel,
to shrug the yoke, come down from bitter cross.

    The President, I noticed, was impassive,
    attentive and indifferent as a *croupier*.
    Not the least fault or fissure of emotion
    troubled the contours of his familiar smile.

Now this is Ancient History.
We live and learn.

The Gadfly was promoted while
Rebels were scattered like a covey of quail
in everywhich direction.
Folding their caps and gowns like Arab tents,
they muttered "tar and feathers," fled.

Now over coffee, steaming rich
subsistence of the academic nerve,
I hear him say: "What we need
is less of milk and honey and more sting.
Things hereabouts are whitewashed. Let us
act. A little water clears us of the deed.
        And what do *you* think?"

I smile and shrug.
I pay the check and plead a class
and leave him talking still,

safe in the shadow of his Great Man,
a trim Diogenes in tub of honest tweed.

12 *Pedant*

Privately, your pencil makes
wry marginalia, doodles at the edge
of noted pages, underlines examples of
what you call the worst excesses.

"Puddles of sentiment!" You scrawl
an epitaph for Shelley and his critics,
being uneasy among the vague Romantics.

"Pope & Swift would have admired
    Bentley & Dennis
if *only* they had understood."
Thus gladly reconcile and make a peace
among the factions of your favorite century.

If I hide my mouth to laugh,
if I yawn, doze while you drone,
if, choking on my imprecision,
I curse you in the language of those years
for "a Blockhead and a Fine Dull Ass,"
I must (in truth) confess

your strictness is like a conscience,
your rigor's like the pattern which
the feet must follow in numbered silence
before they waltz free to real music.

One learns to count before one learns the dance.
One learns to speak grammatically before
one takes the stance of satire and/or praise.

And I have seen the virtue of
your passion for precision.
You teach, by vehement revision,
that labor is a way to love.

THREE STUDIES OF AESOP
For Richard Wilbur

1 *The donkey in the lion's skin*

I take this tale to prove
much that we love and fear
is false when tried by speech,

for only the lion should roar,
as cooing becomes the dove
and a peach is a peach is a peach.

But those whom gestures move
to sail for unknown shores
or taste of fruit beyond their reach,

must take the donkey for
a wise beast and approve
what he was trying to teach.

2 *The raven and the fox*

As usual, the fox is right.
And flattery's a terrible swift sword
and vanity a wound that doesn't heal.

But what was (in truth) the case?
Wasn't the chance that once,
just once, the raven's voice

would be seized by a wonderful tune
worth any morsel of food
and the sight of a satisfied fox?

3 *The tortoise and the hare*

If standing at the finish line
wreathed in flowers and/or smiles
for newspapers is what
counts, the moral's fine.

If such Persistence is correct,
praise the spider and the ant.
Fiddling grasshoppers can't
please Aesop's Architect.

But God knows there's a place
for those who for pure joy
run and fall asleep
while solemn others win a race.

OLD SAWS NO. 1
"A rolling stone gathers no moss."

This is the simple truth: e.g. the rock
of Sisyphus (so lichenless it gleams
like a bald man in the sun) it seems
will never have a moment on its back

to sigh and stretch and feel a fine
green growing like a handstitched lace
among the honored piles in public place.
Few of us can mellow like good wine,

age into some gracious Judgment Day,
in caves as nice as any Plato thought;
but, daily sold and daily bought,
are judged and juggled, roll away

as smooth and nude as grapes on vine.
Still, there's pleasure in the constant dance
of things. Many will sparkle and by chance
a lone stone like a diamond shine.

OLD SAWS NO. 2
"You can't make a silk purse out of a sow's ear."

On the contrary, it appears
that truth is always in disguise.
Take, for example, the careers
of gods in flesh, so camouflaged,

they blend into the texture of
our sweaty dreams of sweatless enterprise,
or those tall heroes who for love
fall on all fours and howl like cats

in heat. This proves the silk
can be converted, you surmise,
but not the negative. We milk
this world (says Wilbur) but we don't believe.

I say that, blest, all water turns to wine.
I say there's more than meets the eye
when Salome, veil by veil, her fine
clothes peels to the essential skin

and bones. There are two thieves.
One of them spits and shuts his eyes.
The other, seeing truth so naked, grieves
and finds himself in paradise.

OLD SAWS NO. 3
"You can't plant peach pits and grow pear trees."

A man is more than sum of all his deeds.

Say that the finest actions could be kept
like flowers pressed in pages, say that doom
is totalled from a column of calm figures,
the dark and light, the services and sins,

until there comes in fire a single answer,
ineffaceable and indisputable, what then?
There are heroes for whom horses wept
and stones, and how shall frail perfume

from antique flowers guard a noble gesture,
though multitudes of ghosts may haunt the tomb?
Grass grows rich where white Adonis stepped,
and from the bones of Orpheus, bright as pins,

poems sprout still like grain from quickened seeds.

THREE CHARACTERS IN SEARCH
OF A NEW DUNCIAD

1 Nostalgia, the Fugitive

I knew a dandy false as a lead coin,
a rednecked cracker called himself a Colonel,
wore spats and gloves, carried a pliant cane,
and left a wealth of laughter where he went.

I know those fops of Jonson and Moliere.
They enter lisping, overdressed,
and speak in foreign accents till the end
when all their cosmic vanities are bared.

What price simple nakedness? You know
the story of the Emperor's new clothes.
Our children snicker at us when we go,
solemn and foolish, wrapped in sheer illusion.

So I salute the dandy and his sin,
the counterfeit, the Colonel whose wide porch,
soft-footed darkies, juleps were untrue.
He turned my grit of teeth into a grin.

2 Milksop, the Poetaster

Pencil in hand, he stared into the mirror on the wall.
He gazed and wrote what isn't poetry at all
to celebrate his bland identity. What waste
to yoke such meager talent to such lack of taste!

3 Fiddler, the Angry Crab

After some eager applause,
he aims to kill. The shining target
waits. "I sincerely regret,"
the archer says, "these brutal laws."
"I am indifferent," the target replies.
"The thing in itself!" the arrow cries.
"To be clever is to be wise."

CELEBRITY VERSES
Figures from the 60's

1

Painting Ann-Margret's
my idea of fun
a sopping wet rainbow
of colors that run
a slithery sloppy
a flowery thing
is pretty Ann-Margret
all wrapped in a ring
of slaphappy shades
and pigments quite motley
no wonder gay blades
pursue her so hotly
till she rolls on the canvas
like a pure artifact
it's kind of a pity
Ann-Margret can't act.

2

Twiggy is leggy and terribly thin
a bustling business & a live mannequin
hustling hairstyles & fashions & maybe a shoe
O living with Twiggy would be living in sin
with a real corporation that's limited too.

Some Twiggy's are wooden & found in the store
in long-legged poses in clothes & the nude
and that kind of Twiggy will never be lewd
no matter how shrewdly a man might implore.

O would she or wouldn't she woodenly wantonly
though skinny give any & than many give more
then doze in her dream & brazenly snore?
Alas the bare truth is Twiggy's a bore.

3

Kim Novak is blonder
than Mother and me
Kim Novak is blonder

than a mother should be
she's blonde at the bottom
and all blonde on top
O no one in Sodom
was blonder than she

Erotic Norwegians and neurotic Swedes
exposed and uncovered with unseemly speed
will blush like brunettes and world will discover
she's blonder than they and blonder all over
it's Kim Novak's secret and she never tells
why she's blonder and blander than anyone else.

4

How does it feel to be Barbara Steele,
your face on the screen, your name on a book?
Does it feel quite unreal to be Barbara Steele
like a cake in in the mind of a cook?

Is it fun when you peel Miss Barbara Steele?
Does she jump for her life like a trout in a brook?
Does she fall in a trance or suddenly squeal?
Does she dance at the end of a hook?

I feel in my bones that Barbara Steele
would not like this bold liberty took
and like other girls (half sugar, half seal)
never leaps without more than a look.

5

Donna Michelle
is round as a bell.

Sing hey nonny ninny
    tit willow to woo
Sing hey ninny nonny
    ding dong & ding dong

She's round and she's firm
and wears a suntan
the color of honey
right out of the jar
she's a round and a firm
and a tough-looking honey

to touch her I venture
costs plenty of money.

Sing hey nonny ninny
sing horny sing ho

She can stand on her head
she can dance like a doll
she can pose on a bed
like Eve before Fall.

Sing Adam and Eve
and a fig leaf for two

And round goes the world
and round goes the sun
so ring out wild bells
for Donna is one
girl whose roundness
I'm happy to tell
is as sound and as clear
and as true as a bell.

Sing hey horny ninny
dong ding and
ding dong

FLASHCARDS

1 To a Certain Critic

Walking in the woods, you turn over a rotten log.
Out from under crawls something very snotlike and pale.
If it could open its mouth and talk good English,
you'd know exactly what you sound like to me.

2 Another Literary Wife

"All I ever really wanted," this pretty woman tells me,
"was a guy with the body of a truck driver and the soul of
a poet.
And look what I got. . . ! Just see for yourself. . . .
An Iowa City Mumbler with a build like Archie Bunker."

3 *One of Our More Fashionable Poets*

His best-dressed lines read like the subtitles
of an old foreign movie in black and white.
His enigmatic metaphors tend mostly to sound
like illegal aliens learning Basic English.

4 *To A Rival Poet*

Lights out in the barracks and always then
a hallelujah chorus of farts commenced,
the least of which was more like music
and sweeter, too, than any two of yours.

5 *Book Review*

I am using your pages
to start wet kindling wood.
Amazing such pale poems
can make a bright fire!

6 *Introduction to Contemporary Literary Criticism*

What Famous Lady Critic actually said
(in Boston on January 18th, 1978):
"If she had only been able to keep her health,
Flannery O'Connor might have made it in New York."

7 *Portrait of the Artist as Cartoon*

Silence, exile, cunning, I resolve to embrace
them gladly, proudly; and then the phone rings
and I trip and fall all over myself
running for it, hoping it's for me,
praying my luck has changed, my time has come.

8 *I Must Have Peaked Too Early*

"Sir, Madame, Person, Occupant,"
the National Endowment addresses me.
"There's still space available and plenty of time
to reserve some of the same for your mortal remains
at the Tomb of the Unknown American Writer."

9 Welcome to the Medicine Show

What I have done here is simply to bottle
some of the natural hatred and malice of poets for each
    other.
I guarantee it will do nothing at all for you.
But it will sure enough shame a hornet or a scorpion.
It can make a rattlesnake laugh and roll over like a puppy
    dog.

10 My Main Confessional Poem

I confess
I am not guilty
of anything I'd care
to tell you about.

11 Worldly Wisdom on My Forty-Eighth Birthday

True, I'll never be rich or famous or beautiful.
But today I still have the good sense to invite you
to come a little closer and kiss my bare knuckles.
Try to ride on my kneecap like a rodeo bronco.

12 Consolation of Philosophy
(for Maria Katzenbach)

Art is long
and I am short.

13 My Grand Strategy

There ain't no good
in a wornout broom
Going to get me a brand new one
and sweep out my living room

14 End of April

Do I really need to tell you
how suddenly light my body becomes
when fallen cherry blossoms smear
sweetness all over my shoes?

15 *Late Night Rain*

Tonight only a timid pest
sprinting away across my dark lawn
like the last drunk guest.

16 *Splitting Wood*

Feet apart   ax at arm's length   over head
I swing downhard now   and easy
falls open a whole length of oak log
freeing the white sweet brief ghostly fragrance
which is really something
                    may   be   every   thing

17 *Same Old Story*

My dancing girls are here to stay.
Though whipped and chased away
like money changers, they
always set up shop again
to take away my takehome pay.

18 *Let It Be Our Little Secret*

All too true that your face
is turning to leathery lines,
but oh-me-and-oh-my the rest
of you shines like newborn.

19 *Since You Asked Me, I Guess I'd Better Tell You*

A perfectly thrilling intensity which can only be achieved
        by total freedom from the boring burden of
    character,

and this closely coupled with the almost complete
        absence of
        even the basic, most commonplace of virtues and
    values,

and all of the above linked together with the explicit and
        continual presence of her irremediable selfishness,

these are the obvious lures that light up a man in the
    same way
flame does the wings of a hairy moth.

20 *Jacob*

Years and scars later
I finally learn
all angels travel
under assumed names.

21 *Easter*

Lord, in your light rising,
pray lift my heavy spirit, too.

THREE MORE SHORT ONES

1 *an epigram by Martial*

To the reader: when you look
inside, you're bound to find here
some good verses, some middling, and I fear
plenty of bad ones. What can I say?
Buddy, it's the only way
a poet can make a book.

2 *definition*

What we spend first of all is innocence
which, after all, we never owned,
but like a borrowed book returned
unread, or like a secret was not kept
but published though the whole world wept.

3 *little tune*

The rent payment's due. Got holes in my shoes.
The world turned upside down. I read it in the *News*.
The color of a sigh is the color of the blues.

THE MARCH PROBLEM

The wind became a green idea.
The crows were out of place.
That color didn't suit their taste
or advance their bleak careers.

The concept started to careen.
They plead a fervent case.
The wind became a green idea.
The crows were out of place.

It was wonderful to hear
them flaunt against their fate;
two shrill ascetics, born too late,
denounced the Technicolor leer.
The wind became a green idea.

TUGBOAT

Blundering behind a white mustache,
a dated handlebar of foam, squat and emphatic,
(One thinks of Teddy Roosevelt, those decades,
and John L. Sullivan who, though he mixed
with shanty Irish taste his bourbon and champagne,
could lick any man in the house.)
graceless as a pelican on the ground,
crude as a jackknife in a realm of swords,
this boat has virtues of its own,
swaggers, not without reason, among
the liners unlikely as birthday cakes,
the ploughboy freighters in straight furrow,
and the lean warships gray as sharks.

Prodigal, the fine ships come and go
like knights to seek whatever dragon,
whatever damsel the dubious horizon hides.
Leaving and the tug's a damn nuisance like a dog
yapping at your heels. Go home! Go home!
Returning, you spy your grave retainer coming,
faithful behind his poor mustache. On land,
out of armor, dragons no more than creatures of dream,
at home, by fireside, to be forgotten.

But now, for one moment, you must say:
"What a miracle is simple duty done!
How crude, how comic, and how rare!"

THE STATUE

The statue
    perched bronzely on a granite slab
    can't bleed. His handsome thrust
    is forward, above the city's traffic,
    amazement and dismay. He leans
    splendidly from a semi-permanent horse,
    one hand poised in spectacular benediction,
    the other occupied with a heavy sword.

The taxis
    circulate precariously around him,
    tilting on shrill wheels. Children
    and nurses in geometric paths
    indulge in ageless fairy tales
    untroubled by that stern profile.
    Pigeons abuse him and many old people
    mistake him for somebody else.

He bears
    all this as well as bronze can,
    and with very little resemblance to
    the delicate and stumbling old man
    who puttered in a garden or played
    with an electric train and yearly appeared
    in all the papers cutting a birthday cake.
    The funeral was elegant and sad, though
    it rained and all the flags drooped.

A plaque
    speaks of stupendous deeds,
    styled in a Victorian rhetoric.
    One, stopping to read it, sees
    the eye-deep agony of hell,
    the vulture angle, wolf's gnaw. But
    the figure is magnificently impervious,
    changes a little as the seasons change,
    and looks best in a diffuse twilight.

WISHFUL THINKING

From falling you can learn the grace
of failing well, from losing rise to be
the agile leaper of the tennis net,
the old king raging in the storm
or, anyhow, the smiler with a knife.

Not everyone can cut a dragon down to size,
be heir to tincan millions or
bed down with a favorite movie star,
slap-happy ever after. In the disaster
not everyone will save his skin.

Lucky in love and war are few
and far between. This scene must end
with many lesser corpses to be lugged before
the lovers can dissolve in clinching bliss;
and many who bear witness wince

when, at last, a minor god appears,
a boyscout with a first-class noose,
to prove the miracle of matchless fire.
The rest must pass like ships at night—
cargo of unhatched chickens, pounds of flesh.

Still, to be beautiful among flashbulbs,
captured by tabloids, might be worse—
never to be able to deny three times
before the rooster crows, never to curse
perplexed successful Pilate face to face.

FRAGMENT OF A TRAGEDY

A messenger,
        guiltless and eloquent arrives
        to speak the rhythms of catastrophe.
        The chorus, formal and self-conscious
        as a football team in a photograph,
        listens and translates in public language.

The Queen
        turns pale, mumbles the usual
        platitudes, and, with the lonely dignity

of a dancer, disappears. She will die.
The old King also must die. He enters
adjusting his fighting gear, awkward in armor

as a duck
on dry land. His sons have all fallen
and his daughters are resigned to fate.
All his generals have vanished. The Army
is moving to the rear with the unerring instinct
of birds going south for the winter.

The King
stops briefly to comment on the laws
of man and nature and the vexing end
things often come to. No god descends.
He shrugs and, as the curtain falls,
salutes. At this point thundering applause.

GOODBYE, OLD PAINT, I'M LEAVING CHEYENNE

From the television set come shots and cries,
a hollow drum of hooves and then,
emerging from snowy chaos, the tall riders
plunging in a tumultuous surf of dust.
The Stage, it seems, is overdue.
My children, armed to the teeth, enchanted,
are, for the moment at least, quiet.
I see the Badmen riding for the Gulch,
all grins, not knowing as we do
("The rest of you guys follow me!")
the Hero's going to get there first.
And as the plot like a lariat spins out
a tricky noose, I shrink and become
a boy with a sweaty nickel in his palm
waiting to see two features and the serial
at the *Rialto* on a Saturday morning:
Buck Jones, the taciturn, Tom Mix
of silver spinning guns and a white horse,
and somebody left face to face with a buzz saw,
to writhe into next Saturday morning.

But how you have changed, my cavaliers,
how much we have had to grow up!
No Hero now is anything but cautious.
(We know the hole a .45 can make.)
No Badman's born that way.
("My mother loved me but she died.")
No buzz saw frightens like the whine
of a mind gone wild. No writhing's like
the spirit's on its bed of nails.
I clench my nickel tighter in my fist.
Children, this plot is new to me.
I watch the Hero take the wrong road
at the Fork and gallop away, grim-faced,
worn out from the exercise of choice.
I see the Badmen safely reach the Gulch,
then fight among themselves and die,
proving good luck is worse than any wound.
My spellbound children stare and couldn't care
less about my fit of raw nostalgia
or all the shabby ghosts I loved and lost.

ANOTHER HAT POEM

I have been trying out different voices
like the fat ladies in old-timey movies
trying on hats in front of the mirror.

I have been taking off countless hats
like the boy in the (James Thurber?) story.
And never keeping any one on for long.

You tell me about William Tell.
I answer that I'll doff them all
in the presence of any honest Emperor.

But that in the interim I aim to continue
making strange faces in funny hats
and hoping that in due time the stranger

in the mirror will choose to wink back
and that on that judgment day we'll know
each other at last for long lost friends.

Meantime better to be alive and foolish
than bald as an apple, silent as a stone—
one more hatless skull with a fixed grin.

CLASSIC GENERALISSIMO

So, finally the emperor was fed up
with the shape of things. His statues in the park
leaned and slouched like beggars after dark.
Imagine that: equestrians with tin cups!

His ribbons wilted. His uniform came back
from the dry cleaner's faded and shrunk.
"Colossal anarchy! All government is bunk!"
Roared the dictaphone behind his back.

He stood up tiredly, buckled on his sword.
Thousands waited underneath his window,
thousands waited for his final words.

He spoke briefly. "Goodness is enormous. War
is a grotesque dance, and life's a puppet show.
Where do all sweets go? How should *I* know?"

THE MOWER

A week of rain has let my lawn run wild:
a prophet's beard, a mob with swarming blades,
except where, here and there, like a bad child,
a lone tongue flutters pure derision.

Well then, it's time for cutting, it appears.
Time to meet force with force, to roll
a keen and leveling weight on ragged sneers,
to snip off foolish tongues and shut them up.

And so I sweat behind my lawnmower knowing
prophet's head will haunt me and these slaves
will own my acres and, despite all mowing,
green tongues will bronx the air above my grave.

VENTRILOQUIST'S DUMMY

Let me tell you a thing or two.
But first you must learn to bear
with stiff ways and a splintery tongue.

It is a terrible thing to be inspired!

Believe me, I'd rather talk
in my own voice even though it is most like
the creak and groan of trees in the wind,
no more and no less. . . .

He with a tongue of raw meat,
teeth like tombstones, joints as free
and supple as rawhide, catgut,
what does *he* know?

I sing you a wooden verse.
I clack and crack my jokes until
you clap your soft palms red

and my two glass eyes cloud
with a miracle of tears.

LETTER FROM A LIGHT DRINKER
"You cannot suck poetry out of the cosmos with a straw."
A. E. FRIEDMAN

One time in the Army I was poor,
too poor even to buy a postage stamp,
a razor blade, a toothpaste tube.
(It happens like that once in a while.)

I had a buddy who would stand me to
a single can of beer at five o'clock.
Dusty, dirty from working, I'd run
all the way from Motor Pool to EM Club.

The thing to do was to sip it through a straw.
It made the beer last longer and
bubbles rose, shining, dancing, in your brain,
and I'm telling you (and you better believe it)

the world turned upside down and glowed.
You might as well have been in China
or in Thule where (they say) ice jewels everything
and on clear nights you can hear the stars

make lucid fugues like a hive of bells.
It was good, it was fine, and I've never been
drunker or happier since or more dazed,
ravished by the riches of this world

and more fearful of my diet in the next.

ROMAN NEIGHBORHOOD

The Institute of Divine Love,
which is just around the corner from
where I'm living, is a mystery.

To me anyway. Nobody
seems to come or go by the locked gate.
No light winks from blind window slats.

It's so quiet it might as well be
another monument, ghosted, cold and dusty,
except for the fact that a brass plate

near the gate with the name on it,
The Institute of Divine Love (in Italian),
looks always freshly polished, gleams

like the cared-for brass of bank buildings.
There is a high wall, and along the top
they've strung a long thick strand

of barbwire. But what I like
about the Institute is
that the wire is old and sags

in disrepair, and, best of all,
there's such a jungle of roses
(I can imagine it) on the other side

that the bushes have groped over the wall
and all that green weight has overwhelmed
(like dreamed-of surf) the sad wire.

That's as it should be. I call it
neighborly for roses and barbwire
to keep a silent mystery together.

TEA WITH EXPATRIATES

In the Villa Aurelia so many dishes

come with a cup of tea
that I might as well be a juggler
as to try to drink it and at the same time
keep track of the cookies and sandwiches.
O what a confusion of china and little spoons
is civilization trying to be at ease
        with itself!

Through the tall windows I can see
the sprawl of Rome below, the old stones
extravagantly burning up the afternoon.

My host complains the convent that's nearby
wakes him at six with morning hymns.
Hostess says that plumbing is a problem
and that our Embassy is grossly overstaffed.
Butler, in a white coat and pink
from a fresh shave, moves on the soft feet
        of a stalking cat.

Two French poodles, like a pair of toys,
gambol on the lawn of carpet.
There are no children in this house.

The city glows below in slowly fading light.

Much as I am pleased
I haven't dropped or spilled
or broken anything yet
I have an itch to go.

I want to go down into that last light.
To drink it, splash in it, bathe in it.
I want to be deaf in the noise of it,
the shrill and always ringing,

laughing, cursing, crying, singing
chaos of the city whose inhabitants go forth

and multiply like loaves and fishes.

EXCURSION

We wandered in a half-lit chilly dark.

Half-lit because the light was sieved
through chinks and cracks and holes.
Chilly because it was already winter.
The tombs, in fact, were closed;
but *lire* seem to be the magic key
to anything this side of heaven's gate.

We stumbled in a half-lit chilly dark
and saw their implements,
(symbolic, of course and nothing like
Egyptian ones I've read about,
real ships, real swords, real beds)
carved into the living rock.
And we saw their frescoes too,
the sad, wide-eyed, two-dimensional people
we could scarcely believe in,
but there they were, their dark eyes answering
no questions, telling no secrets at all.
There are times when even lovers share this look.

We moved into another chamber
where someone giggled.

"Well, they sure knew how to live,"
our host and guide, a Philadelphian,
Harvard- and museum-trained, said.

What glowed on the walls was *erotica*,
the daydreams and the night thoughts,
the pinned-up wishes of the ancients.
One in particular caught our eyes,
(the light fell on it best).
A slave on all fours is the lady's couch,
and she, thus mounted, lies
back, knees high, to receive

("receive," I believe is the word we use
nowadays, the proper euphemism)
a standing lover
whom nature or art has hugely gifted.
She is no more of flesh and blood
than a playing-card queen,
but still her false face is alive with joy.
She seems to like her shaky perch.
Her lover is much more solemn and intent,
gripping a mighty instrument.
The slave is stolid in his pose.
What is he thinking? God knows.

And we, the creatures of another culture,
one where truth is seldom in the nude,
whose tombs are plots of silence
and whose dreams are fugitive as spies,
to be caught and shot at first light?
Someone has giggled, somebody joked,
and now in separate privacy we creep
into a crazy house of mirrors
where the self, disguised, assumes
a shiver of swift lewd poses
like a gambler's shuffled deck.

Does it seem strange to go to the dead
for the facts of life?
Orpheus, Virgil, Dante, Christ
descended in the dark and stirred
the troubled bones. And we,
with all hell in our heads,
must follow or go mad.
"Love, let us be true . . . ."
old Matthew Arnold sang,
who couldn't have meant what he said.
Or maybe he did. . . .
I have seen a Victorian gentleman's
boot-remover made of brass—
a naked woman whose spread legs
catch and pull off the boot.

We move along and pretty soon
are outside in the open air again.

"Places like this have a kind of truth
that the public monuments conceal,"
an archeologist says.
"Boy, I wouldn't want to be that slave,"
the shy sociologist tells me.

But what I like best is
the classicist from Vassar.
She's suddenly bright-eyed and wordy
like somebody with a fever.
"Until I went down in these tombs
I never really *believed* in ancient times."
She babbles of bones and artifacts
(meanwhile avoids the subject of
the tomb assigned to human love)
and bounces like a little girl
on the back seat all the way home.

OUT ON THE CIRCUIT

Waking alone with a hangover in the Howard Johnson
        Motel
I could as well be in Denver or Miami or Emporia
and could as well be (I like to think) a travelling
                salesman at least
or maybe a conventioneer, a straggler from some
        conference
on, let's say, new procedures and guidelines in
                modern corporate accounting.
But I am not, I cannot be; I was here, wherever I am,
to read poems and to talk about poetry with students
and my head is a booming buzzing ache of words,
words, words, my own and other people's, said and
        unsaid.
We wear the order of the laminated cliché like a
        convention badge.
        Lordy   Lordy   Lordy

Waking with a terrible hangover in Howard Johnson's,
head a hive, bowels a kennel, legs spaghetti,
eyes a tattered sunset, hands as broken wings, face

114

a full moon in daylight, lonesome and
   irreparable,
I stagger with the heavy shame of my lazy tongue
which, before it became this thing of leather and fur,
was lively and sleek as a pair of semaphore flags.
Message as follows: I have left undone those things
   which I
ought to have done etc. etc.
And there is no health in me.
And there is no reply.
   Lordy   Lordy   Lordy

It is always worse than I remembered, worse than I
   imagined.
I have worn out my welcome of words like a limp deck of
   cards.
The last pale one-eyed Jack, a common prankster,
relinquishes the kingdom of the blind man with one
   wink.
Kings and queens glare like grandparents. The Joker rings
      hateful bells in my ears.
All the aces have shaken off the dust of my shabby
   sleeves.
Only, inside coat pocket, the coat hanging loose on a
   chair,
directly in front of the mirror that I carefully avoid
   greeting,
inside that coat's pocket, clean in a crisp and windowed
      envelope,
the printed check waits patiently for me, virginal and
   wise.
Ah, money be light and music and vintage wine,
finally sweeter and stronger than the kisses of beautiful
   strangers.
I have cheated no one but myself. I have stolen nothing
      of real value.
For this sweet charity I'm pleased to sing like a crow or a
   bullfrog.
   Lordy   Lordy   Lordy

Reduced now to debit and credit, I rise from a rumpled
   bed
in the almost certain hope that a shower and a shave and
   a clean shirt,

the sweet taste of toothpaste on my tongue and teeth, will charm
and distract the prophet into ignoring
        the motionless mountain,
and in the faith that this first swallow of whiskey in a
        plastic cup
will drive all my ghosts to ground and welcome again
        some charming guests.
I shall be cured of every symptom of doubt and dejection.
I shall decide that my Howard Johnson room is only
        cheerful.
And I shall be only cheerful in Denver, Emporia, Miami.
Ready and able to shuffle the old deck and deal under the
        table.
Willing to flash the latest clichés like expensive cufflinks.
Rich now in my coat of many colors, the reassuring check
        fitting
                comfortable and heavy like a gun in a holster,
I raise my glass to share a toast with the stranger in the
        mirror,
to rejoice together in the inexhaustible resources of self-
        deception,
beyond the deepest dreams of decent salesmen and cost
        accountants.
See how my hands are steady. Now I know how it is to
        live forever.

MANIFESTO
For RHW Dillard

to begin again

after a long time
and many promises
not to say anything
not to add another voice
to the damned cacophony
cacophony of the damned
makers of verses
spinning prayerwheels
of speculation & gossip
fast & faster

till the words are gone
all voices howl & moan
becoming at last
the humming tune
of a whirling top

o prayerwheels & tops
who is able
to translate you

who reads you
loud & clear

avoid poets
as once ancestors
carefully avoided
lepers with little bells

evade eloquence
a beggar's palm
hungry for coins

elude logic
a clenched fist
to break noses

how many times
facing a waste
of blank paper
have I said
nothing no not one
not one least leaf
falling to flame or
flagging the spring's
first & final heat
not one southward
surge of birds
nor even the song
of their returning
not laughter & tears
neither body dreaming
nor mind gambling
nor spirit kneeling. . . .

no swore I   no   nothing
under sun & moon
will make me begin again

who has wrestled angels
feeling flesh wither
who has danced with demons
drunk on all fours
knows what I mean
who for all honor
has yet said
instead of keeping
holy silence
has left unsaid
when words were kisses
knows I mean well

who too much has seen
of naked untruth
too often heard
the old songs pass
like dirty pennies
from palm to palm
he reads me
loud & clear

yet have I today
shameless gone forth

o damned cacophony
what have I done

confess
I bought a notebook
and a new fountain pen

to begin again
ring little bells
to begin

The pen is red.

III

Lovers & *Others*

"No, No, Orlando! Men are
April when they woo, December
when they wed. Maids are May
when they are maids, but the
sky changes when they are wives."
AS YOU LIKE IT   IV, i, 146–150

RAINY DAY

It is raining hard today and the girls that I teach
come to class, lightly over the wet lawn, barefoot.
A corner of the room sprouts a garden of umbrellas.

One stops by the door to dry her feet,
hand propped on the frame to keep her balance.
Her foot is small and soft, delicate yet sturdy.

One small sturdy hand pressed against the door frame.
Small sturdy suntanned legs. She stands on one leg
and crosses the other as simply as a bird.

I am pleased. All this time and I didn't even know
you had a foot, young lady, flat sole and little toes
to go to market with or run squealing all the way home.

I am troubled, too. Off *my* balance, I feel
the intimate shiver of the elders in the garden
when young Susanna gently let her garments fall.

God knows I am past thirty. And knows
I have a job to do and children of my own to feed.
Let me disappear. I shrink and vanish

into a camouflage of bright umbrellas.
Now they have turned into mushrooms,
magic toadstools glistening with rain.

And in just a minute my students will run past me,
skimming the wet grass on swift feet.
Won't one of you stop and pick a toadstool?

And sleep forever in a shining spell?
Though the world goes gray, be always pink?
Though old men lust, smile in your sweet dream?

A bell is ringing. I find my hands are opening
a book. Rain falls outside and I look
into a flowering of blank pretty faces.

I have seen one face, so beautiful it made me sing,
fall to ruin in a cracked looking glass. And I have felt
time print crow's feet at the edges of my own eyes.

So much, then, for the glitter of rain, the shining lawn,
a garden of toadstools, faces like flowers and one bare foot
I should have kissed for joy. "Let us take up where

we left off yesterday. . . ."

SUMMER STORM

In such a wind as this the trees
toss their heads like women
in a pique of bitter disappointment.

In such a wind the clouds
go wild, stampede, dark and shaggy
as buffaloes or prophets.

"Whip me such honest knaves!"
howls the professor, highlighted,
theatrical behind his lawn mower

amid the wink and crack of thunder
and lightning as the rain
comes flashing like a thousand swords,

like Agincourt's clouds of arrows.
His child inside the house looks out.
"The bears!" he cries.

"The grizzly bears are running away
with the sky!" He's delighted.
Not every day the zoo's turned loose.

His wife from the bedroom sees
the professor soaked and stamping.
She smiles. He never knows when

it's time to come out of the rain.
She tosses her head like the trees,
shakes free her careful hair

and stands by the window of the dark room.
"Take me with you," she whispers
to the wind. "Let me go running

young again in the whips of the rain.
Take me with you." (to the wind)
"I promise I'll be good."

A MODERN FICTION

A lion with a fiery mane,
    roaring and raging came,
came to a field where roses grow,
where roses in perfect stillness grow.

The lady was pale as the snow.
    The lion leaped in her eyes
like brightness stolen from the sky,
like the fire from the heart of the sky.

She held white lilies in her hand,
    wore violets in her hair,
hair as yellow as a full moon and
robed like the lilies in her hand.

—He has come from the burning sky.
    He's wild, she said, but I
will put out the flame and learn his name
and teach him manners when he's tame.

—The pale moon has tumbled down,
    grumbled incredulous lion.
The moon has found a soft new bed,
ice and snow on a field of red.

It was the lion who fled,
    fearing that walking cold.
—How marvelous to see, the lady said,
the sun go running, red and gold!

FIGURE STUDY

I The Photographer to the Nude

They say the Zulus or some such tribe
(I forget which. Let them simply be

123

dark, our shadows, our consciences.)

believe in no such thing as a straight
line. Believe? They can't conceive
of it. Their houses are all round,

and their implements are curved,
and if you try and civilize them—
put them to ploughing fields, building

fences or just going from here to there—
they achieve it all in gracious circles.
There's truth in that. Nothing I know of

is perfectly straight unless a hand
touched and twisted and tormented it.
The wheel's the noblest act of man.

Be still, be natural, my moon.
Be all the snow of the world's dome.
Be the high sea dreaming in a bed of stars.

And I, ducking behind a dark cloth,
I'll disappear like magic and become
a Zulu with an uncorrupted eye.

II The Nude to the Photographer

There's a wilderness in women
you haven't dreamed of. We are
dark continents, not sea, not snow.

The panther moving like a swimming thing,
the tiger like a creature all on fire,
we know by heart and fear.

The world's a heavy weight, the moon's
a lonely journey in a vacant sky.
Flesh stumbles for its crooked mile.

What is beautiful? An arrow finding
the target's eye, a keen plane
smoothing rough wood to a level,

and clay rejoicing in the kiln.
Choirs of stone sing from a well-made wall.
And God's best gift is the human hand.

For God's sake don khaki and pith helmet!
Bring axes, ploughs, bulldozers, and
conquer, colonize, convert!

Bring light to cast some shadow.
Bless me with angles and I'll be
yours in two dimensions for forever.

SOME WOMEN

"Talking about women means talking about the darkest part of
ourselves, the undeveloped part, the mystery within."
FEDERICO FELLINI, *quoted in* Playboy

"If you take off the makeup, I'm ugly."
JEAN SHRIMPTON, *quoted in* Pageant

1

Cheerleader
Bouncer of basketballs
Stern keeper of homeplate
She ran on beautiful strong legs
around my dreams for a full year
bright hair streaming behind her
and laughter like golden apples
daring one and all to muster
energy to master her

I am sorry
I was not the one.

2

She was a hearty
        country girl
blonder than peaches & sturdy
        as a Percheron
could climb trees like a squirrel
        & plow like a grown man
& laugh like an acrobatic angel
        in all weathers

Once we lay down on the sweet grass
        in a cool shade

leaves dancing to their own whispers
& a bluejay scolding both of us
    with a woodwind tongue

—Don't leave your coat and hat, she said,
'cause we won't be coming back this way.

3

Sensitive
she moved easy to tears
for example by
sunset woodsmoke seashells kittens
poetry from The Romantic Movement

I see her yet in a white hat veiled
swan-graceful in our rented canoe
cool fingers coaxing a guitar

I can hear her singing *Greensleeves*
Barbara Allen & *Go Away From My Window*
& always *The Golden Vanitie*

And when I sank her in the lowlands O
she laughed louder than the 3 witches
she gnashed her teeth & cried out
a foreign legion of four-letter words
    like little prayers

4

Remember how we went to church together
from thence to the Palm Court of the Plaza
where we drank milk punch and tried to talk
theology (of all things!), joy and suffering?

Will your wide eyes brighten now
and what will your eyebrows ever do
if I stop fooling long enough
to tell the truth? Tell the truth
in love, St. Paul said. I would not
hurt you with a lie to lie with you.

I would, however, I confess,
cheefully, gently undress you altogether
and, equally cheerful, gentle as can be,
hold tight to altogether while we fell

126

down breathless miles of waterfall
and rock-and-roll of roller coaster rides.

Into your circus tent I'd creep
without a ticket stub or conscience
to spank my palms in loud applause
for the shining bareback rider.

Your smile is worth waking for.
The ample pleasures of your city
(o whiter than Paris) worth a Mass.

I here confess I suffered that Palm Sunday,
a stylite burning painless in the Plaza
where words like buzzards soared and sailed.

I think you are made of milk and honey.
I live in a desert of hot rocks.

O Lord, here I hang by bad jokes,
like thumbs, just to make her laugh.
Will she pray for me next time she's kneeling,
light candles, wear a birthday suit?

Listen, to make your clear eyes brighten
and widen with waking wonder, I
shake hands with suffering and rejoice.
I will bear witness in the unknown tongue
though every theologian crow and though
your eyebrows rise higher than hawks.

5

Why do I sing and celebrate the mad wild girl?

She whose long hair was dark and live as snakes.
Her eyes were brilliant hard and lost
like agates on the playground of the spring.
Whose laughter sudden and mysterious and coarse
as a cat's tongue. Oh and her body was a bow
without an arrow, a lute without one string.

Loving was always to wrestle in the dark
with later sobs and rustle of chilly sheets.

Where are you going? I called from the shore.
My answer was in salt and sting of wind.
She sailed close to the wind, heeled and vanished.

127

I could not heal her. I swear no man could.
I think one day she'll learn to grin all right,
when she's a painted doll calm in a satin coffin.

To make the best of it, I cried *Bon voyage!*
Hiked and shrugged my shoulders like a soldier's pack
and went off like a bumblebee to girls like flowers
who smile and sway in veils of sun and rain.

She drank straight wormwood, cut her teeth on bark.
Frantic she ran from packs of yaps and snarls.
And in her dreams she was a willow tree.

Let wild dogs take her then.
Let her bones rest in lonely peace.
I'll find another piece of milk and honey,
sweet milk, dark honey, bread and wine.
I'll pick up all my marbles and go home.

Why do I wake now in the middle of a dream
to smoke and pace and curse her Christian name?
Why shiver again for kisses ghostly cold,
shudder at skulls, all tongueless, bald. . . ?
I pinch to see if I have turned to stone.

She never even said goodbye to me,
whose heart lies broken at the bottom of the sea.

6

blond dancer in a cage

Silence is darkly plural.
Sounds and noises die at once.
I listen to them fade and go.

I have known many silences,
of midnight, high noon, of dawn;
then the scream of a saw, cry of an ax,
of the least breath of breeze in dusty leaves
might have been purest music.

I have heard the bright new songs
of birds and buds proclaiming spring
and the drunken hum of swarming bees
and the drumtaps of my marching heart. . . .

I have longed for perfect silence
with a truly bitter thirst.

Frost in my veins and nerves,
dying in bits and pieces,
I doze and dream like a lazy snake.

Your sudden music batters, breaks the spell.
I open my eyes and see you dance like water,
sweet water, fresh water, light dazzled, poured
over edge of lip and rim to flash in a rush
and shatter like glass in the sun.

And now you bathe in a shower of old gold,
I wake to the joy of a song and dance
I never dreamed of in clamor or quiet.

I blink, I stretch, uncoil and rejoice,
o bright and wholly singular girl!

Be still my broken bones.
Be still for as long as she dances.
Let me listen and be silent.

If ever she would falter and fall,
I will kiss her awake with all my wounds
and clang a fine tune on my chains.

7

Wee-doggie! Let me die this way!
She cried at the top of her voice.
It was, of course, our very first time,
and the first is the best, they say.

But soon she was in a different mood
when she sat fully dressed on the bed.
I assure you it was all a dream, she said.
And I: *I only dreamed you in the nude.*

(after the French of Paul-Jean Toulet)

8

girl in black raincoat
sing about her here & now not later
there are always things
better not recollected in tranquility

who never a daffodil could dance
nor even like the poorest grass
all o watered with sweat & tears
fed with sweet marrow of dry bones
cut clipped rolled & edged
can sway to the whims of the breeze

yet she did dance a little while
ah & her least whim or glance
could wake from cold hearts more joy
than cascades of silver dollars
from the finest slot machines

so let her gambol while I still gamble
betting it all on life love light
while the old dealer in a pair of dark glasses
shuffles to show the ace of spades

see her dance to the edge of the world
& look down though warned against it
to count stars & see them glitter & shiver
Goodbye! she cries & chooses
doffing darkness & flashing head over heels
brightness forever as she takes the long fall
      See you later. . . !

goodbye girl
I lose you lose he she it loses
though death's the old man who shuffles & deals
yet will grass grow & daffodils will dance
to be resurrected in tranquility
o she's long gone &
I pause to praise her here & now

9

She is so beautiful in the morning.

She wakes from her dream like a bird,
a ghost of the dew and the cold.
Yawns then and opens eyes
the color of cloudless skies.
Smiles brighter than brand new pennies.
Laughs like little bells in light wind.

Face to face with her amazing dawn,
who will deny me my civil rights

to stamp my hooves like a snaredrum?
Who says I can't salute
when the rooster of my thighs
cries *cockadoodledoo*?

10

When all our songs, both yours and mine,
die with breath to drown in dust,
will feet of unborn children rock and roll
like thunder over our thin roof of earth?
Their cries will shatter songs to smithereens,
as dandelions are scattered on the wind.

Well, what's in a name or a song
when the sun is only shining
and the wind is rife with seeds?

Dust is dancing in a waterfall of light,
see, now! through my window panes.
We read your poems and talk around them.
They are writing love poems for you,
as is meet and right to do, and I,
I look toward light and see a dance of dust.

So every song and dance must end and then
begin again. Another throat and other lips,
hair like honey and eyes more brightly blue
than the breezy, kite-crazy skies of early March. . . .

Come what April and let my skull grin.
I too have danced as I swivel now
in my teacher's swivel chair like a toy.
You sip your milkshake through a straw.
I believe the world is sweeter than they say.

11

Good cloth coat, wool kneesocks, and a bright-
            colored hairband
of ribbon, and her clean hair firmly brushed
            to equal shine and gloss,
she enters my office with a thin sheaf of poems
            and teasing eyes.
Cool she is, and long before the word was either
            cliché or metaphor.

Sits most proper and polite, neat and straight
                    of hem, smooth of knee.
And she listens to the clumsy words I rattle
                    and roll like dice,
making none of my points, crapping out like a born
                    gambling fool.
She is newly married. Her young husband is a
                    stranger to me.
"Yesterday," (smile) "I shoved an ice cream cone
                    right in his ear."
"What did *he* do?" "Oh, well, he put his cone
                    in my hair and then
I had to wash my hair all over again."
                    Dance for me now
pale in the steamy shower, soft and graceful,
                    with teasing eyes.
Let them flash and fleck wild colors, then
                    veil themselves too.
Once upon a time in Casablanca, with only
                    short time to learn,
I made burning choices of veiled women by the glint
                    of their eyes alone.
Perhaps that was good enough, as good as any sign
                    of inner fire. . . .
In her mythic poems, blithely she tosses aside
                    kneesocks and all,
and, simplified to flesh and flame and chaos,
                    wields a wicked knife.
She's drunk, dark, savagely possessed, a high
                    priestess of blood.
Demonic with rich nudity, she turns poor men
                    to pigs and toads.
Yet here she sits, calm and composed, while I
                    grope for image clusters.
In movielike orgies fat clusters of grapes
                    bleed for your fingers.
I notice suddenly that your own fingernails
                    are bitten to the quick.
Lady, young lady, I wish you well with all
                    your poems and dreams.
My teeth are chipped and my knuckles are pairs
                    of loaded dice.

I am too old for teasing and gambling now.
Win or lose,
you'd cry to be a tree and I'd be only bones
for my mad dogs.
Go, then, be young and happy, lighthearted, be
patient and gentle
with your young man and all your clusters
of ancient wishes,
lest knees go raw from prayer, your eyes become
red from weeping.
Child and woman, young bride, my lover
never and forever,
don't make me add my days. I have won more
kisses than scars,
and truly I can count and gloss more scars
than you have years.
Yet just as truly I can be only grateful
for this game.
I dance you in my dream. You tame and teach
my songs and sorrows
to rejoice. Wounds are not wisdom. Love is
an ice cream cone.

12

apology

A bright and clever poet
has not only written but published
a poem about my wife.

He celebrates
the formal calm and grace
she wears like a magic cloak
when she plays the golden notes
of Bach, Frescobaldi, Dowland,
spinning only the finest sounds
from her Velasquez guitar.

Clearly this is a poem
I should have written.

Oh never doubt it for one minute
I have dreamed a poem for you
a thousand times and a thousand times
have tested my skill and failed.

Now I am only green envy.
My fingers are ten fat thumbs.

How will I ever write a poem for you?

You who are all my music,
whose dancing is the only dance I know,
whose eyes and smile make all my light.

You whom I choose and hold
in dream and nightmare, fire and flood,
ever and always in flesh and blood.

You whom I would choose to praise
though all guitars were kindling wood
and every clever poet were mute.

13

Having tested & tasted
your fine flesh with all 5
clumsy eager hungry senses
(though lightly gently slightly)
I am now more than 5 mouths

O I taste & touch the savor
of 7 seas & the burning sun
and (just there) the cool light
of a new moon & the old song
of long & lonesome journey

Now I may believe in the world
I think the world may be round
and firm & free & easy to love
I rejoice in all your round worlds
I know where you are silk & spice

7 seas to cross & 7 gates too
to conquer a tall castle
Lance & spur & sword I ride
amid roses & barbwire of briars
to kiss you while you dream

Sweet dreamer o my slow smiler
if you wake not if lost & tossed
I sail right over the edge of earth

consider this   Until I sleep for good
my 5 & foolish grins are only yours.

14

Warm sun and sweet wind
new leaves greener than memory
dogwood more delicate than brides
tulips lax as after love

Warm sun and sweet wind

I lie in the sun to think
I think that I might be happy
if you came to me here and now
wearing sunlight o sweeter than wind

I lie here drunk with dreaming you
Come to me now and I will cover
completely you with a robe of kisses
Be still as a flower while I whisper

my secrets to your secret places

THE WINDOW

On summer evenings at a certain time,
and always the same as if by the clock,
she cast her shadow on the shade,
and huge she loomed like a goddess
painted against the yellow window shade
to strut, to stretch, to dance
and finally with a light, coy leap
to take to her bed and cut out the light.

We grew up as she grew old.
From awe and secrecy and shame
in the breathing dark we fumbled
into laughter and at last
indifference. By day she was
only a plain girl, cheaply dressed,
living lonesome in an ordinary room.
By dark she was a figure from a dream.

Language was what she taught us,
paradigms of curve and countercurve,
songs of the moon the sea, the dying sun.
Truth also. How each shadow is
a blest disguise and how the heart,
broken, glitters in ruin like a box of jewels.
Laughter we came to, how foolish and how small
was all the sum of our desires and hers.

Later—where did she go?
married? another place? another town?—
it was over for good and high time
to think about it. If a shadow is
wholly beautiful, what of substance?
Oh, I do not mean poor flesh. I mean
the dance of spirit to a fitful music,
sorrow, desire, love's wordless mystery.

BATHING BEAUTY

The sun, this morning
scored for trumpets, blares
over the sculptured gestures of
bathers in brief costumes.

They are untouched.
Only the gulls and children fly
for joy to that holy noise.
Older we warm by the tune

like the blind by a burning
fire. Cat-sleek, curled
in knowledge of herself,
dozing in the dazzle,

she has caught my eye.
I see her on a scallop shell
or lounging in the perfect lines
of a Matisse.

O Suzanna, I'll
stand on tiptoes, breathless
among the frozen elders. O
Judith, here's my head

my heart my four limbs
and my balls and all
(O Ruth) my alien corn.
She stretches, sighs, and seems

to be asleep. I shut my eyes
to hear the gulls and children
sing. I hear my voice
wailing at an ancient wall.

The sun, all trumpets, blares
and the sea is falling, falling
like the walls of Jericho
whose waves are tongues of dust.

STRIPPER

Don't pity me.
While you sit in darkness,
stare and sweat and itch,
I dream I bathe in light.

Darkness is the night
and your eyes are stars,
more numerous and bright
than Abraham's seed.

I alone in the light,
lighthearted, am high lifted,
bird on shining breeze.

Do not judge me
and I'll judge you not.
Why should I damn your eyes
when I own them one and all?

True, at times I shiver
and sometimes even catch cold
with nothing much for cover
but veils of dust and smoke.

But when I greet my mirror
a bored and aging stranger laughs
and my heart staggers like a drunk.

Oh not for pity or pleasure
I peel myself like a grape.
Nor for a trick of loaves and fishes,
to be divided and devoured whole
by your lost lonely tribe.

I dance alone in starry skies
to prove that dying stranger lies.

SHARDS FOR HER

You are the spirit dancing in seven veils.
(I watch you from my bed of nails.)

You know the deep places of the sea.
You know the dance of fountains in the light.
You are the spirit dancing in seven veils.

You breathe the keen air of mountains.
You have seen the glare of heatstricken, silent places.
(I see you from my bed of nails.)

You bring me the green heart of springtime.
I taste. It is bitter and good.
You are the spirit dancing in seven veils.

You are all my light
when I wrestle with angels and demons.
Come, love me on a bed of nails.

PROPOSITION

Times when my mind is curled
on itself, a sprawling cat,
a sleepy Persian by the fire . . .
When your least gesture signals love,
what can I do but purr?

How are you haunted most?
Someone, next as a shadow, goes
always with you even in dreams,
blowing a chill breath on your lips,

peering from the cave of your looking glass
like yellow eyes in the dark.

O close your troubles like a book.
Come to me now and bare your smile,
my Cheshire, until, all vanishing,
you are brightness pure and simple.
Leave plots of silence for our ghosts.
Let's choose the music of this world.

INVITATION

In a bad time
my five senses are
spies in disguise
who say old prayers,
undress in the dark
and die at dawn.

It's a bad tune
to march to
while baldest words
wear wigs and pure lies
jangle in fine purses
of pig's ear.

It's a bad dream
where nothing is strange
except what is
only simple.
We live on the kisses
of enemies.

See the bad man
kill with his smiles.
He teaches how to dance
at the end of a rope.
Whatever he can kiss
he claims he owns.

O it's a bad time
to make promises
when the words have lost
all salt and savor,

when the finest shining
is of fixed bayonets.

Now's our last chance
for reaching and touching—
to undress bold
in bright lights and hold
each other captive
in fragile chains.

There's a good dance
whenever you lie still
with me and for me.
It's the best time
for singing on key
of sorrow and of wordless joy.

FALL LANDSCAPE WITH TWO FIGURES

Time did not stop for us. It ran
reckless in the stream we walked by
and free in the blood of our locked hands.

There was not mercy in that autumn sky,
the color of a bruise, that warned
of cold to come, that promised storm.

There was a hill where a few sheep
huddled like fallen clouds.
There was a flaming tree, but the hill was steep.

Behind us the town fell over the brink
of the horizon. Steeples and substantial brick
vanished as if the known world were the wink

of a lazy eye. We were alone.
We stopped by a rock that too much time
had sanded nude as bone

and talked inconsequentially of things
done and undone, of crowds and voices,
remembered hours and uprooted things

we named with love. It was strange
in that failing scene to sit on rock
and talk while time and the season changed.

TWO TALES OF LOVERS

1 Guardian

Who walked on tiptoe,
one finger to his lips to signal hush.
Efficiently converted
a kingly palace to a gray museum.
Any wonder, then, he wailed
to find his pretty statues gone,
their empty pedestals grinning like
a cast-off set of false teeth?

2 Shipwreck

They sailed in mirrors,
floated on wild seas of delight
and foundered there.
Dawn finds them surfaced,
spent, bemused and beached.
"My cargo's gone," he moans.
"My heart," she says,
"went down like captain with the ship."

A PARABLE OF FOUR SOWERS

1

She was a dazzle.
How her words flew!
Like strange birds.

Who could capture
the fury of their wings
or their fierce songs?

Where I've planted
nothing will grow.
Nothing prospers.

Let dark birds come
now and find me.
Pluck out my eyes.

2

My joy was joyless.
Her bright smile was
a pair of shears.

So rare her flesh!
But at my touch
she turned to stone.

All I can harvest
is crop of bruises.
Mouthful of chaff.

Pity the hunter
whose bowstring is slack.
Limp arrows in quiver.

3

My love was rich.
Golden her body.
Coins for her eyes.

My love was treasure.
I was a pirate.
Faulty the map.

For crown I wear
thorns. For bread
I taste fists.

Find me a willow.
I'll show that tree
how to bear fruit.

4

My love lay fallow.
Dust on her lips.

Green in my eyes.

My love was sleeping.
I stormed her dream
like a tall tower.

My love's a garden.
Wild children grow
calm in her hands.

My love is holy.
It would be a prayer
to praise her in words.

MARTHA GRAHAM: *Appalachian Spring*

Our blue mountains are vague as smoke. In April we
    dream we
are awake. Our dreams are pink and white like dogwood
and as sweet as rock candy.

Then the Devil comes walking like a bear on his hind
    legs,
and his fiddler sets everything to dancing. O Martin
    Luther,
O Jack Calvin, can't you keep those tunes out of my ears?
    In
April, in May, the Devil makes his music like a fat
    bumblebee
in the flowers.

Thank the good Lord, the long dry summer days come
    soon after.

VALERIE BETTIS: Streetcar

When the Elders found me I was not Susanna.
I was transfigured, gored and tossed in their eyes. When I
    felt
what they were thinking my body turned to stone.
    O Susanna, don't you cry for me
    In New Orleans, land of dreams

Take me in your hands. I swear I'll come to life again. I'm
just like a fish out of water, a birdie in a cage. Take me in
    your
hands and all of me will smile and dance for you.
    Pretty birdie, sing me a tune
    In New Orleans, land of dreams

My lips taste dust. But, ah, my flesh is cool and fragile as
    the rain.
I am the Sleeping Beauty. No one can ever wake me. Be
    kind . . .
    O Susanna, don't you cry for me

CARNIVAL POEM

I see completely through you, lady,
dark lady, though I see darkly.
To travel in the Tunnel of Love
I take your hand and you lead me
to the Funhouse of Mirrors where I
learn by heart your ways and moods.
You make faces while I grow fat and thin,
grotesque, a clown beside your curves.
Faced with so many, how can I choose one?

Round go the rides and the merry-go-round,
clad in lights and laughter and music.
We blow smoke rings at each other.
Frog, fish, bird, who am I now?
Priestess, princess, forest nymph,
dancer or dreamer, which do I dare
to touch? And if we seek to kiss,
which one will turn from that to stone?
Will you vanish like the Witch of the North?

Mouthful of cotton candy sweetness,
armsful of highpriced, hardearned dolls,
cradling that tawdry brood of children
not your own, you do not answer me.
When I walk through mirrors, I enter green
fields in a sudden garden of stained glass
where you are dressed in only sunlight.

And I name you Eve. Come take my hand.
Kiss me and I may yet prove to be a prince.

APOLOGY

Berryman wrote sonnets and published them, too,
to tell it all, to tell it all like Petrarch.
And so would I. So would I, except

there's much I do not dare to tell myself
and just as much that I'd tell you and no one else.
And you have secrets that I'll never live to know.

So be it. So be. "So go be," as they say
in the West Indies. Those coffee and chocolate girls
who walk like lovely ribbons easy unrolling.

Except, too, there's no story here to show and tell.
The light facts fly up and away and cry like gulls,
and the sea leans and tilts with or without them.

So let me confess this much and no more.
You are my Carribean, salt and sun, richer than China.
You are coffee and chocolate to my taste, your breath

the breeze off distant islands, sweet and strange.
You have secret harbors, and your touch is fever to my
    flesh.
Your laughter is fresh water. Your kisses are ripe fruit.

Give fame then to all surviving sonneteers.
Sad chains for the few who promised China.
Smile for the man with only wide eyes and a fever.

What can I do but babble this nonsense and report
prodigies which no one else will believe, except
I believe in you always as I believe my own name.

MESSAGE SENT IN THE CLEAR

Beyond words now, I look into your eyes,
feeling the lines at the edges of my own
crinkle and crackle with urgent messages.

I do not know what they are telling you
my ragged scars, chevrons of time. You read
dark cryptography, top secret strategy.

True or false, who can say? Who speaks
of those things? What does a Pvt. with a pair
of dry socks and a whole cigarette care?

Victory and defeat, the lucky live to dance
in the streets. Yet lucky also the soldier with
fire for cold hands and a good clear day to die.

Damn it all! I shut my eyes and think
mysteries are forever and we are here and now.
You are my mornings, and while I live I am

happy to bathe my wounds in your light.
Thoughtless, I know your lips are only sweet.
I trust my hands and believe your body's dance.

INSTEAD OF A LOVE POEM

There's no sense in any of it
paper envelopes and postage stamps

neither for love nor money
and why else would a sane man

not even for a pat on the back
from our Pres-i-dent
not one billion pairs of palms
pink and glowing with applause
would be worth it

would be worth
my hand and yours
your pink and mine
or any of your glowing

I pat you and I make
my own applause

so
lie back easy love
let stars in your eyes

be all our light
here now and always

you can trust me
not one word of this
no jot or tittle
no least whisper to repeat
in verse or prose

I'll keep our secret secret
and save a postage stamp

SAME OLD STORY

I will be dead
and you will be dead.
It's a natural fact.

If I start to shiver
may I warm my hands
by your white fire?

Listen, snowmaiden,
my sleeping princess, while
I begin to shimmy and shake
and make a kind of lonesome dance
with the rattle and jangle of bones.

The maestro approaches the podium.

(Surely you remember Milton Cross?)

What you fear most of all
is not the inevitable custard pie
nor banana peels and whoopee cushions
nor even the laughter of
the dark gods of your dreams.
I think you fear that one wink
will signal your shame to the world.

Turns and bows to the audience.

I never saw anyone grin
back at a grinning skull.
Did you?
Why be proud and lonely?

Trust me.
If you ever catch cold
let me be your boyscout
with a miracle of matchless fire.

Come let us wink together
and laugh in the light and the dark.

You say why.
I say why not.
O tedious dialectic!
I know a dance for two.

The maestro raises his baton.

CAN'T WE BE FRIENDS?

She writes him at his home address:
"What I mainly want to do
is fuck you in front of your wife.
I'd like to make it in the presence of
all the women you've ever been to bed with.
I want us to do it before an audience composed
of every woman you have known!"

He frames a reply with some care:
"Naturally I understand the nature of your feelings
and I appreciate your sincerity and your candor,
but believe me when I say I'm not at all sure
these things can form the ideal foundation for
a viable student-teacher relationship."

NEGOTIATIONS

DIPLOMATS GROPE
TOWARD PEACE
the headline blares
boldly allowing that
not even diplomats are
essentially different from
the rest of us. In spite

of cutaway coats, striped pants,
attaché cases and limousines,
poker faces and impenetrable
language, nevertheless
they, too, fumble and fiddle,
rustle, wrestle, shimmy, and shake
and shiver in the search for that ultimate shudder
followed by a dazzling smile
which passeth all understanding.

—Diplomacy is not
the answer,
I answer simply.
Negotiation gets me
simply nowhere with you.
Look, you're already smiling,
and you haven't given up
a single inch of territory,
made one concession
or offered to reduce
your openly hostile posture of
self-defense which I call
frankly provocative.
What do I have to do?
I ask you. The translation
must be faulty. I will not
go and fly like a kite.
Or whistle tunes
like a Gulf shrimp or wait
patiently until the Nile
flows south and scholars
forget how to make footnotes.
Further resistance is folly!
SURRENDER NOW OR ELSE!
Be prepared for anything
rougher than rugby or a cat's tongue
or a car wash or British woolen
underwear. Something memorable like
Ben Franklin's shocking kite string.
Clearly much is still being lost
in the translations. Your knees
aren't quaking. Your lips remain
irresistible. Your eyes
brighten beyond my understanding.

HEY, CAN YOU GIVE ME A LIFT?

Body be laughter. . . .

My horseless carriage
my old engine
stutters and dies
a lemon off the lot

Quit stalling
Go tell her right now
how her eyes and what her walk
how much darker her hair than
and whitest her bare back must be

Tell her that
twin fine horses prance
her admirably magic coach
directly to the prince's dance
Say her voice
is like clarinets
all ebony and silver

Body is laughter. . . .

What chance
has he got whose heart
is a toy drum
whose music is made
by tin whistles
and whose head is
irreparably pumpkin

Too many miles
on my map of flesh
I cough and stammer
rattle and rumble
and end up standing
by the side of the road
raising a bald thumb
and very best smile

Home is wherever
you are going
wherever you want to
take me to. . . .

TAHITI MAMA, WHO LOVES YOU?

"Wisely," she writes, "I have just turned down a date
with a gentleman recently on the cover of *Time*
magazine."

Nixon? I wonder. *Ford? Rockerfeller?*
Who else has there been lately? "Jack Nicholson,"

my wife, patient with my enormous ignorance, says
as she bends over the ironingboard. "That's who!"

Too bad, Jack, boy. When she walks into a room,
groins react like the Guards to "God Save The Queen."

She used to work for *Cosmo* and now writes poems.
"Maybe she could have written a poem about it."

"I doubt it," my wife says. "I don't imagine
a fling with Nicholson is exactly a poetic experience."

Color of honey, breasts like Tahiti, more curves
than the road from Roanoke to Grundy, Virginia.

Eyes dark with secrets and bright with promises.
Lips that shine wetly, *just* like a *Cosmo* girl.

Too bad, Jack. She writes poetry and letters
about fine and fancy times in New York City

and all the people, famous, glamorous, notorious,
the celebrities she either goes out with or doesn't.

Too bad, George. You live by a river (far from the city)
where seagulls cry like children lost in fog.

I believe she is really the goddess Fortuna in disguise,
fickle and faithless, desired and wholly desirable,

like that seashell woman out of deepest ancient dreams
who makes wisdom look like somebody's plain little
    sister.

"I'll never be on the cover of any magazine,"
I say. "I'll never travel to Tahiti or any place like that.

"Dark, beautiful women never write poems about me.
Guess I'll never have any luck or magic again!"

"Tough shit!" my tall and beautiful wife replies,
folding my shirts while the steamiron sighs.

151

"Why don't you write a poem about that?"
Lucky in love, laughing and scratching, I swear I never
will.

SINCE IT IS VALENTINE'S DAY

Nothing but trouble from now on (you said),
a rawhide string of Februaries.

My stomach growls agreement.
I have arrived at the age of half-truths.

Since it is Valentine's Day, I remember
bodies and beds, the breath and flesh

of others, each one a perfect stranger now.
I have lost their names like marbles on the schoolyard.

For better or worse, in sickness and in health,
self-incrimination now replaces self-delusion.

I count your sum of scars and subtract my own.

Your eyes, brighter and bluer than many,
are more like eloquence than sorrow.

Try as I will, when we touch,
I shrug the old bones and cut my losses

into the shapes of stars, of hearts and flowers.
When you say doom, I hear a blooming rose.

BELLY DANCE

Once I told you how
(I heard it from somebody
who swore that it was true)
the belly dance began
in ancient Egypt to instruct:
an *exemplum* for innocent brides.
It was regularly performed
at wedding parties and
given most serious attention.

I argued then (the sophist of
half a fifth of bourbon)
that it was the right thing,
proper that such knowledge
should be passed on,
decorous that it had to be,
typical of our times that nowadays
the belly dancer has to live
in the brittle scrimmy world
of nightclubs, of misplaced
erotic daydreams, of sex
in a strange greenhouse growing wild.
Where the talk went from there
I don't remember, only that,
as usual, my tongue wagged
like a lazy semaphor until
somebody else wedged in a word.
Talk will be the death of us
yet. But, anyway, imagine
my astonishment to find you now
alone in our bedroom dancing
in front of the mirror.
You have folded your nightgown
down from the top. Your breasts
are bare and free and fine.
You have folded your nightgown
(an aquamarine and gauzy thing
I have always been amused by)
below the eye of your navel
and, from where I am standing
behind you, unseen,
In a neat line across the twin curves
of your hips. What a joy
to my eyes, first and last,
is the shape of this woman
naked! I love you,
but what in the world are you *doing?*
Arms overhead, a kind
of standing odalisque, you are
swinging hips to left and right,
a pure delight in awkward motion.
A twentieth century woman
tentatively tries an ancient dance.

Now is the time for words
and I am tonguetied. I rejoice
and laugh at the same time.
Then I step into the mirror
and you blush and are angry
because I am laughing at you.
We are a long way from Egypt now,
my love. No palms, no pyramids,
no weeping crocodiles to give
proper setting for performance.
I only want you as you are,
my belly dancer. Take me
with a grain of salt.
Believe nothing except this:
As the round world moves, the moon,
the tides, so you. Like them
you are the subtle rhythms
my blood dances to. My heart
sings (wordless) to your tunes.
Let idle talk be damned!
I like the way you move
without a spotlight or snaredrum
or any historical precedent.
I take you in my arms for good.
Why be so proud and lonely?
Let's do a dance for two.

THE BED

When I was younger
much more solemn than now
and couldn't watch a leaf fall
without an archetypal twitch
and every apple was original sin,
and we were new to each other,
still shy and guarded, I
wrote a poem about waking up
after the wrestle of love
and then the lonely sleep.
I wrote about the first light,
about the breathless moment when

one discovers one and one
make two. For better or worse
there would always be the two
of us to share one bed.

I can't recall it now.
I think that I compared
us to fallen angels.
And then that fancy simile
dissolved and doubled and
love was an old-fashioned dogfight
from the First World War
and lovers were Spads and Fokkers
looping, spinning, falling
in crazy trails of smoke and flame.
Then it became a shipwreck
and the world a forlorn beach
where, half-drowned, we raised
our heads to find each other
still alive and kicking.
I believe we were disappointed,
in the poem at least,
discovering that even in survival
being alone is a luxury.
I know how foolish it is
to try to make a drama of
a good and simple thing.
Still, it does take awhile
to lose oneself enough
to measure one's delight
by another's mystery.
What a waste of time
to wait so long to learn
that love is purely a dance!
All that I wrestled with
in darkness and in light
was not angels, but myself.

Now after love we fall
easy in each other's arms.
Now sleeping is to float
on calm and moonstruck seas.
Now when I sleep I dream
of gardens where apples are

simply beautiful. I pick one
and I offer it to you.
It's sweet and good to eat.
Now when I wake I smile
for joy to find you there.
One bed is surely plot enough
to hold our several ghosts.
And there is ample space for two
to ride the liferaft home
from shipwreck into harbor.

A TOAST FOR THE BRIDE AND GROOM

I raise a glass of wine,
but how shall I confine
in words the music of
this captured light? Love
dances free, will not keep still.
Can grapes, so crushed and chill,
contain a calendar of sunny days?
Can empty cups be filled with praise?

I know a list of famous cups,
once tasted, once turned up
and drained to the last dregs,
could make you shiver like the legs
of a new colt. Down on their knees
dropped Circe's drinkers. Socrates
proved bitter can be sweetest good.
There's one that turns the wine to blood.

There's another of that kind
that once made water into wine,
and that's the one I wish for
now. Glass, be a metaphor.
Wine, be symbolic, and my toast
be shy and sudden as a ghost.
What's unsaid is all history.
"Our glasses brim with mystery."

FEELING GOOD, FEELING FINE

After pleas and persuasion, all the frozen
uniform gestures of prose,
having said my say, my hup and hip,
the closeorder rhythms of dismounted drill,
I have come back alone to naked verse—
a man singing and dancing in the shower.

God knows I have known the deepest cold,
have slept with snow and waked to wind,
to shining wind blowing all the white way
from old Siberia. We huddled then
by little fires, blew on blue fingers,
called coffee more precious than blood.

Goodbye boots and parka. Oh, so long
to the clumsy soupbowl of my helmet.
Pack and rifle, belts and gear all gone,
I hang my dogtags and towel on a nail
to lightheaded, lighthearted, stand
in rosy steam and sing your name

and mine again. O what is a man
singing offkey with pure joy,
dancing loosejointed calypso and highlife,
with no more weight to carry now
that one slight, brightly astonished heart?
Go ask somebody else. I am alive again.

I who was cold to bones am warm and clean.
I who was heavy as a walking bear
am bare of all burdens and briefly free
of fear for now and do not give a damn
who hears my voice and laughs out loud.
Clown or shorn lamb, I have my pride.

But if you happen to laugh, I'll be happy.
And if you choose to clap your hands,
I'll shower you with roses and breathe steam.
I am unarmed. I do not even have a knife.
The letter kills, the spirit giveth life.

George [Palmer] Garrett
   (1929—
      Florida
      — Princeton

The *Sleeping Gypsy* (1958)
Abraham's Knife (1961)

King of the Mountain (1958)

In the Briar Patch (1961)